The Mighty Message
of
MARK

by
Thomas J. Smith

ST. MARY'S COLLEGE PRESS • WINONA, MINNESOTA

To a group of my friends
who met on Thursday nights.
We searched the Scriptures and found,
to our surprise,
what we were supposed to find:
An Experience of Community

Photo Credits
British Museum, cover; Bob Combs, 62, 212; Berne Greene, 20, 193;
William Hedrick, 116; Vernon Sigl, 167, 213; David S. Strickler, 265;
Wallowitch, 45, 92, 117, 137.

Library of Congress Card Catalog #73-81824
The Mighty Message of Mark © 1973
by St. Mary's College Press, Winona, Minnesota

Contents

Acknowledgment

The author wishes to publicly express his dependence on many kind and helpful people for the completion of this book. In a general but very real sense gratitude is due to the People of God for their rapidly increasing interest in studying, praying, and appreciating the Scriptures. It is safe to say that the Holy Spirit, among other things, is "breathing" in the direction of the Scriptures and that many people are following that direction. For this interest, I am grateful and hope that *The Mighty Message of Mark* may provide a greater understanding and a deeper faith in those who read it. More specifically, I would like to thank the people who encouraged me to research and write this text, particularly "The Thursday Night Discussion Group." A special word of thanks is due also to the 1973 Senior Class of Assumption High School in East St. Louis, Illinois, a group of young men who studied this material before it was a book. Most of all, gratitude is due to Fran Hart for her continual encouragement in preparing this text, her valuable assistance in researching the background material, and her critical evaluation of the written copy. Without her help, *The Mighty Message of Mark* might still be an idea in the back of my mind. To my typist, Margie Jones, my public expression of appreciation is a small acknowledgment for her great patience and ability in typing and discussing the content of this book. And finally I would like to thank the Publishers for their confidence in this project and their personable assistance in seeing it to completion.

Why Mark?

Some things last a long time. Even in this age of rapid change when fashions, ideas, movements, and inventions move over quickly for new fashions, ideas, movements, and inventions, there are some things that remain rather constant. Heroes come and go, oftentimes lost in the maze of heroes of the next generations. But some personalities have lasted, proving the relevance of their message in many different societies and in many different periods of history. Jesus of Nazareth is one example of such a personality. Jesus has lasted a long time.

It is true that various ages in the last two thousand years have viewed Jesus from many, sometimes conflicting perspectives. These changing perspectives are understandable: A culture influences the way the people view just about everything, and as the culture changes, the people rearrange their way of looking at things. The significant feature about Jesus of Nazareth is that he and his message have survived these forces of changing history. And it looks like Jesus is going to make it to the twenty-first century as well.

What is it about that Jew who was crucified that has such power and influence? Why has his popularity spanned the centuries? It's those questions that this study will attempt to investigate. The vehicle for examining this influence of Jesus will be the gospel of Mark; we will return to the source, to as close as we can get to Jesus himself, to seek out answers to the questions about the remarkable popularity of Jesus.

The choice of the gospel of Mark is made for a number of reasons. It's considered by most Scripture scholars to be the earliest gospel, the one written closest to the actual events of Jesus' life. It's also the shortest of the gospels, a mere 677 verses. But there is another reason for starting with Mark: Mark wrote his gospel with Gentiles in mind. A Gentile is anyone who is not a Jew and that includes most of us. As a result, this evangelist made fewer references to the Jewish Old Testament than did Matthew and Luke. Not that Mark didn't recognize the Jewish influence on the life and message of Jesus. He knew Jesus was immersed in the Jewish way of life, just like Americans are immersed in the American way of life. There's no way of avoiding that kind of influence. You grew up in America or China or France, and your environment played a great part in making you what you are today. The same was true of Jesus, and Mark certainly admitted it. But he was a good writer; he tried to communicate what he knew and what he believed in the best way he knew how. And since his primary audience wouldn't understand the references to the Old Testament (they weren't familiar with it), he decided to skip many of them. Matthew, on the other hand, was writing primarily for Jewish people and could fill his gospel with Old Testament examples and forms of expression. As Gentile Americans in the twentieth century, we would probably find Mark's gospel easier to understand than Matthew's.

And Mark is also a straightforward writer: He simply says that his account of the life, death, and resurrection of Jesus is a "gospel." Of the four gospel writers—Matthew, Mark, Luke, and John—he is the only one to call his writing a gospel. That title means his efforts are a proclamation, not a biography. He's not going to give us a blow-by-blow account of what happened to Jesus of Nazareth; he's just going to proclaim the importance of Jesus.

The word "gospel" has a history all its own, and Mark knew that history. It was used by the Greeks; it was a victory cry, an announcement that a Greek army was victorious over an enemy. If Alexander the Great defeated the Persian army in a battle somewhere in the Middle East, he spread the news around the Greek empire by runners. These poor runners hustled from town to town and made the announcement of the victory. "Hey, listen everyone! We beat the Persians! Alexander led the battle, and we won!" Then they would run off to the next city. That's what a gospel was—the good news of a victory.

Mark took the word with that meaning and applied

it to Jesus. In effect, he shouts out right in the very first verse: "Hey, listen everyone! Evil is defeated! Jesus won the battle! Rejoice!" It's winning the high school state basketball championship—and then some. It's happiness after a struggle at home—and then some. It's the happy birth of a new baby—and then some. It's drinking a six-pack with friends—and then some. That's a gospel, it's good news. The good news in Mark is that Jesus is risen, and he's still with us. He hasn't left us; somehow he's still present.

The purpose of this study is to discover the significance of Mark's gospel. The format will be quite simple: The gospel will be divided into eleven chapters. Each chapter will then be subdivided into three sections: The first section will answer the question, "What's Happening Here?" in which we will look at the gospel text itself and provide a commentary about the meaning of that text. The second section will respond to the question, "Where Did This Message Come From?" and here we will try to acquaint ourselves with background material needed to understand and further appreciate the meaning of the message. In the third section we will ask, "So What?" and attempt to draw conclusions from the text and relate them to the twentieth century. Before each chapter is studied it's important to read the corresponding verses in Mark's gospel. At the end of this book we should be better informed about the content and the purpose of this gospel, and more knowledgeable about the process by which this gospel took shape. Hopefully, the picture of Jesus will also become clearer, and the events of his life will inspire us to become better, more authentic Christians.

The comments about the gospel of Mark in the following chapters are not presented as the "final word" on Jesus or the gospel. Scripture scholars are constantly finding new insights and more exact interpretations of the gospels. But what is offered here is reliable: Many Scripture scholars, both Protestant and Catholic, would agree with most of what follows. The *Jerome Biblical Commentary* provided much of the information used in this book, and the *Jerome* is a respected source of Biblical commentary. Although the overall outline and main themes of the Gospel seem to be permanently established, we need to admit that further studies may indicate the necessity for revised interpretations of individual texts. This continuing revision is to be expected and encouraged, since true Christians are constantly seeking a greater understanding of the meaning of Jesus, and one way to meet that Jesus is through *The Mighty Message of Mark.*

Getting Started

Mark 1:1-13

CHAPTER 1

The beginning of the gospel of Jesus Christ, the Son of God.

As it is written in Isaiah the prophet,
"Behold, I send my messenger before thy face,
who shall prepare thy way;
the voice of one crying in the wilderness:
Prepare the way of the Lord,
make his paths straight—"
John the baptizer appeared in the wilderness, preaching a baptism of repentance for the forgiveness of sins. 5And there went out to him all the country of Judea, and all the people of Jerusalem; and they were baptized by him in the river Jordan, confessing their sins. Now John was clothed with camel's hair, and had a leather girdle around his waist, and ate locusts and wild honey. And he preached, saying, "After me comes he who is mightier than I, the thong of whose sandals I am not worthy to stoop down and untie. I have baptized you with water; but he will baptize you with the Holy Spirit."

In those days Jesus came from Nazareth of Galilee and was baptized by John in the Jordan. 10And when he came up out of the water, immediately he saw the heavens opened and the Spirit descending upon him like a dove; and a voice came from heaven, "Thou art my beloved Son; with thee I am well pleased."

The Spirit immediately drove him out into the wilderness. And he was in the wilderness forty days, tempted by Satan; and he was with the wild beasts; and the angels ministered to him.

What's Happening Here?

Mark starts things off backwards. He begins with his conclusion. These first thirteen verses are a prologue, an introduction which states his main theme. In a sense, the rest of his gospel is a repeat of these opening lines. It's as if you would begin a speech, for example, like this: "The Beatles were the best musical group of the past ten years," and then go on for the next twenty minutes repeating that idea and trying to prove it. Mark is using a similar approach in this prologue.

This evangelist calls his account of the life, death, and resurrection of Jesus a gospel. The following 670 verses will be good news inviting the reader to rejoice. Mark then tries to explain *why* we should rejoice. Jesus is the Messiah and the Son of God, the one person the Jews had been waiting for all these years. At the end of the gospel, Jesus will be called "Son of God" again. There, Mark puts those words in the mouth of a Roman centurion at the foot of the cross. Just about everything between this first verse and that admission on Calvary is leading up to that centurion's proclamation. It's a true prologue: The writer states the conclusion, then develops his story to explain what he means and winds up with the same conclusion. During this process of development he hopes that the reader will agree with him by the time he gets to the end.

Since Mark is writing for Gentile readers, he avoids many references to the Old Testament. But he couldn't

avoid Old Testament ideas completely. In fact, it's probably impossible to eliminate all traces of Judaism from
Jesus. As a result, Mark makes an immediate allusion to
the Old Testament prophet, Isaiah. He wants to show in
this prologue that John the Baptist had a special role to
play; he was the forerunner of Jesus, the man who was
supposed to prepare the people for Jesus. Such a person
was referred to in the book of Isaiah. An example of a
similar thing today could be the role of the advance man
for a music concert. It's his job to set up the arrange-
ments, organize the publicity, sell advance tickets, and
try to make sure there's a crowd when the concert takes
place. John the Baptist was the advance man for Jesus.

The confusing angle to it is that neither John nor
Jesus seemed to be too sure just who the other guy was
and what they were trying to do. Remember, Mark wrote
this gospel years after the actual happenings; he had the
benefit of hindsight. It's hard to tell really what actually
happened when John saw Jesus, and what they said, and
who called who by what title. This is not a biography of
Jesus; it's an interpretation of the meaning of Jesus. It
almost seems here in the opening passage that John thinks
Jesus is the prophet Elijah come back to life. The Jewish
people at this time were expecting Elijah to return and
to continue his preaching. John apparently knew that
Jesus was going to do something special, and the greatest
thing he could think of was the return of Elijah. He could
not think of Jesus as God, and at this point he couldn't
even think of Jesus as Messiah. He just didn't think that
way. An American would have a hard time thinking the

same way a Chinaman does. John the Baptist thought as a Jewish prophet, not as a Christian.

John was a true prophet in the tradition of Jeremiah, Isaiah, Amos, and the others. He told the people to repent of their sins and change their lives. "Look out," he says, "you people are not living up to the faith. And you better get ready now, because someone is coming who's really going to put it to you." Those who accepted John's message were baptized in order to show publicly that they really did want to change their lives.

When Jesus appeared one day, he too wanted to receive John's baptism. The vision that Mark describes was seen only by Jesus, and it once again is full of Old Testament themes. The point here is that Jesus is the fulfillment of Jewish hopes, an idea that will receive further development as the gospel proceeds. The reference to the "dove" might help in understanding this message. The "dove" is a symbol of the whole nation of Israel, somewhat like the eagle is a symbol of the United States. Since the dove is present at the baptism of Jesus, the implication is that all of Israel is summed up in Jesus. Another aspect of this baptism account which could clarify the meaning of the passage is the reference to Jesus coming out of the water. This coming out or exodus is a reminder that Jesus repeats and improves upon the first exodus when the Jews crossed the Red Sea and escaped from the Egyptians. So once again, Jesus fulfills the Old Testament and re-enacts within himself the history of the whole nation of Israel. But all of this is known only to the reader; it's a secret to the people of Jesus' time, since the vision, as Mark presents it, is seen exclusively by Jesus. According to Mark, the real identity of Jesus is kept secret until the centurion proclaims on Calvary that Jesus is Son of God.

After his baptism, which begins Jesus' public ministry, he heads for the desert, the place where the Jewish nation roamed twelve hundred years earlier, before they settled in Palestine. The number forty signifies a long time. There in the desert, Jesus is tempted. It's a battle between good and evil, and after considerable struggle, good wins out. This theme too—the conflict between good and evil—will recur over and over again in the rest of the gospel. Each time, just like here at the beginning, Jesus will triumph over the evil.

Where Did This Message Come From?

The gospel of Mark was probably the first one written. Most scholars believe that this account was compiled and written in Rome about the year 70. Some researchers think an earlier date of composition is also possible. The important thing is that it was not written right on the spot, as Jesus was experiencing the events. And since it was the first gospel, it seems that the other gospel writers, particularly Matthew and Luke, borrowed from Mark's account. They apparently had Mark's version in front of them as they composed their gospels.

But Mark didn't just sit down one day at his typewriter and start from scratch. He had materials in front of him too, written resources as well as the memories of eyewitnesses. Scripture scholars say that in the years between 30 and 50 there was a long written account of the Passion story (without the Resurrection appearances), and this account explains why the Passion passages in the four gospels are so similar (though there are differences too). Mark also used a number of pamphlets in putting together his gospel. These pamphlets were collections of stories related to various aspects of Jesus' life. One seemed to contain a number of the miracle stories; another concentrated on the parables. In certain aspects, the process of writing the gospel was similar to doing a term paper. Mark had to look things up in other sources and then put them together.

He had another advantage also. Many people had well-developed memories in those days. They had to, if they were to remember something important. Books were very rare and not everyone could read anyway. But they were not ignorant people. They would memorize. In fact, one of the features of a disciple was to memorize what the teacher said. A *rabbi* was a teacher in Jewish society and his pupils, or disciples, would learn from him by repeating back the exact words the teacher would use. As a result, their memories were very good. Therefore when Mark talked to people who were disciples of Jesus, he could rely on their testimony, because the ability to give accurate and complete testimony was one important feature of discipleship.

Mark had at his disposal then both written and unwritten resources. He was a true author, however; he had a specific purpose and felt free to use the materials in front of him to develop that purpose. That's why some parables, for example, will basically be the same story in Matthew and Mark, and yet they will illustrate very different points.

As an author, Mark was close to a genius. The sixteen chapters all fit together, building to a climax, with opposition growing as the story progresses, and the disciples becoming confused and misunderstanding Jesus constantly. Put into a modern movie with Mark doing the screenplay, it would probably be a very intriguing character study of the central figure Jesus and an exciting picture of the conflicts in society. The gospel of Mark is a compact but marvelous, representation of the spirit and the message of Jesus.

It is good to recall as you read the gospels that we do not have a biography here. There would be many more details about Jesus' life, if it were a biography. It's helpful to remember three levels of development of the gospels. The first level is the actual historical event. Something happened in Palestine in about the year 30 A.D., and what happened revolved around the life, death and message of Jesus of Nazareth. But there is a second level which complicates our reading of the Scriptures. This is the level of the experiences the early Christian Church went through. In other words, by the time Mark wrote in 70 A.D., there were thirty-five or forty years of history to Christianity.

The problems this primitive Christian Church had are reflected in the gospels. For example, John the Baptist had a devoted group of followers. They did not go over to Jesus right away; they stayed with John. They even considered themselves disciples of John after the Baptist was beheaded. Fifteen years later they might meet Christians, disciples of Jesus. They would talk and compare ideas and practices. Perhaps they would get around to the topic of baptism. The Christians had baptism and so did the disciples of John. What was the difference between these baptisms? And in fact, who was greater, John or Jesus? They were both teachers and both were obviously good men. This comparison and conflict was very real in the early Church. When Mark wrote his gospel he was aware of the problem, and that's one reason why he clearly draws a distinction between the baptism of John and the baptism initiated by Jesus. He also makes it very clear that John prepares the way for Jesus, but that Jesus is certainly the greater of the two. Mark does it that way in order to try to resolve the dispute about who was greater, John or Jesus. The point here is to demonstrate how the experiences of the early Church community influenced the gospels. The gospels, in other words, tell us much about Jesus, but they tell us much about the first forty years of the Christian community as well. The difficulty arises in trying to determine when Mark is writing about Jesus directly and when he is writing about the early Church.

Then to complicate matters further, there's evidence of a third level of experience reflected in the gospel, and that's the level of Mark himself. He adds his own interpretation to the events of Jesus' life and of the Church's life. He may rely on the written material he has before him and on the evidence provided by eyewitnesses, but he doesn't just copy that material. He forms it, pulls it together, and adds his own thoughts. He shapes it, using a style that is distinctively his own. He chooses the language. In brief, he puts his special stamp on the final product.

In understanding the gospel then, it's beneficial to know what level Mark is referring to: whether he's writing an historical account of the actual events in the life of Jesus or whether he's considering a problem the early Church is facing or whether he's making an editorial comment, interpreting those events in his own way. Oftentimes, he might be referring to all three levels at the same time, or at least, within the same sentence. It makes reading the gospel more complicated, but it also opens the door to a greater richness of meaning when a person views the gospel from those three angles.

Perhaps an illustration would help clarify what is meant here. Suppose a person says: "The first astronauts landed on the moon on July 20, 1969." That would be the first level of comment—a statement about an historical reality. Then the person adds: "The moon landings have created considerable discussion in the following years about the advisability of our space program. Was it worth the money we spent?" That's an example of the second level of comment—problems caused by the landing and further experiences of people related to the initial project. Then the person adds a third level of comment like: "I believe the astronauts have provided man with a modern example of courage, skill, and adventure." This observation is a personal one, an individual reflection. It is another dimension.

Mark's gospel of Jesus has a similar three-fold structure, although at times it's not very clear to us living in the twentieth century. But a little patience and study will open up the many meanings of the text for us—as Mark wanted it to do.

A final word here about inspiration. Inspiration is the technical term used to describe a Christian's belief that the Bible is also the word of God. There have been volumes written, many theories proposed, and centuries-old discussions attempting to explain what this inspiration really is and how it works. For our purposes, it doesn't seem necessary to recount all those theories. It is sufficient to say that if we can discover what the human author, in this case Mark, meant when he composed his gospel, we can believe that God meant the same thing. Most theories about inspiration would accept that position. If we can discover what the human author really meant when he wrote, we can be relatively assured that the message from God is basically the same. A big problem arises in discovering what the human author was saying; it's too easy to miss the message. And if we miss his message we also miss God's message.

Inspiration implies a certain degree of faith. Without

that faith, the gospels may be interesting testimonies to the life and death of Jesus of Nazareth, but they can never be what the authors intended them to be. Mark was writing to and for believing Christians; it is an account flowing from his faith in the divinity of Jesus and the importance of the Christian message. That faith leaps out at the reader from the pages of the gospel. But it's a faith that cannot be forced; the reader will have to face that question himself and answer it himself. What do you think of Jesus of Nazareth? Who is he? What does he want of us? Mark has answered those questions and he wants to share those answers with us. He hopes that we will agree with him.

So What?

For many people around the world during this last part of the twentieth century, something seems to be missing. Perhaps the same could be said about all people during each century. The history of man seems to be a history of people searching for something—call it happiness, peace of mind, joy, satisfaction, doing a job well, call it whatever you want. But that desire for something is always there.

This present period of time with its mass communication and its almost overwhelming excitement also exhibits this great desire for "something more." Many teenagers express this longing when they admit that they are simply bored with just about everything. School may be

20

boring; home-life may be boring; even going out with the crowd can become boring. What can I do to make life more exciting? Some look for a job, some want to continue schooling, some seem happy steady dating, others try drinking beer, and some get into the drug scene. Why all these attempts? Because something seems to be missing in the way things are right now.

Even those people who honestly maintain that they are happy now will admit that in the future their life situation will probably change and the way they live now, the things that bring them happiness now, may not be with them in the future. In other words, we generally experience a rather disturbing level of insecurity in our lives. Usually the people who have been able to overcome that insecurity (most often by accepting it and not fighting it) stand out in a crowd. They are the confident ones; the ones who are not defensive and who do not put-down others. But it seems that many young people are searching for that confidence and that happiness, searching but haven't quite attained it. The same could be said of many older people.

The popularity of "Jesus Christ Superstar" and the expansion of the Jesus Movement indicates a renewed interest in the person and message of Jesus. It seems that some people are finding help in their search for "something more" by looking to the hope expressed in the mission of Jesus. True Christians have always felt that way.

This prologue to the gospel of St. Mark quietly introduces that hope to the reader. Jesus is baptized and then moves into the desert where he struggles with the powerful forces of evil and overcomes them. Those destructive forces are anything that holds back the comfort and the challenge of the reign of God. Those powers call themselves war, hatred, prejudice, selfishness, exploitation and death. Mark maintains that Jesus provides an answer to these forces and that when the reign of God extends itself completely, whatever is evil will be wiped out. It's that belief which forms the basis of Christian optimism. To be a permanent pessimist is impossible for a Christian. A Christian can be described as a person with fundamental hope.

Where is evil today? How does the struggle between good and evil take place within society and within individuals? Do we really believe that good will triumph? These first few verses of Mark's gospel introduce the need for baptism and the assurance that good is winning out over evil. Baptism is needed to remind us that we too have the power to contribute to evil—we hurt people, we cooperate in policies which take advantage of others, we tolerate and promote injustice, we fail to love our God and our neighbor, and we have many excuses. Baptism reminds us that there is another way. We can be forgiven, and it's possible to contribute to good—to justice and charity, to hope, to love, and to peace. There is another way!

It's a question of attitudes and of attitudes leading to action. If, for example, we think thoughts of peace rather than of war, we are more inclined to act peacefully. If we trust others rather than be suspicious and aloof, our relationships will be more loving. We will be contributing to good rather than to evil, and we will be aligning ourselves more completely with the message of Jesus.

CHAPTER TWO

What More Can You Expect
From a Crowd?

Mark 1:14—3:6

1:14

Now after John was arrested, Jesus came into Galilee, preaching the gospel of God, [15]and saying, "The time is fulfilled, and the kingdom of God is at hand; repent, and believe in the gospel."

And passing along by the Sea of Galilee, he saw Simon and Andrew the brother of Simon casting a net in the sea; for they were fishermen. And Jesus said to them, "Follow me and I will make you become fishers of men." And immediately they left their nets and followed him. And going on a little farther, he saw James the son of Zebedee and John his brother, who were in their boat mending the nets. [20]And immediately he called them; and they left their father Zebedee in the boat with the hired servants, and followed him.

And they went into Capernaum; and immediately on the sabbath he entered the synagogue and taught. And they were astonished at his teaching, for he taught them as one who had authority, and not as the scribes. And immediately there was in their synagogue a man with an unclean spirit; and he cried out, "What have you to do with us, Jesus of Nazareth? Have you come to destroy us? I know who you are, the Holy One of God." [25]But Jesus rebuked him, saying, "Be silent, and come out of him!" And the unclean spirit, convulsing him and crying with a loud voice, came out of him. And they were all amazed, so that they questioned among themselves, saying, "What is this? A new teaching! With authority he commands even the unclean spirits, and they obey him." And at once his fame spread everywhere throughout all the surrounding region of Galilee.

And immediately he left the synagogue, and entered the house of Simon and Andrew, with James and John. [30]Now Simon's mother-in-law lay sick with a fever, and immediately they told him of her. And he came and took her by the hand and lifted her up, and the fever left her; and she served them.

That evening, at sundown, they brought to him all who were sick or possessed with demons. And the whole city was gathered together about the door. And he healed many who were sick with various diseases, and cast out many demons; and he would not permit the demons to speak, because they knew him.

[35]And in the morning, a great while before day, he rose and went out to a lonely place, and there he prayed. And Simon and those who were with him pursued him, and they found him and said to him, "Every one is searching for you." And he said to them, "Let us go on to the next towns, that I may preach there also; for that is why I came out." And he went throughout all Galilee, preaching in their synagogues and casting out demons.

[40]And a leper came to him beseeching him, and kneeling said to him, "If you will, you can make me clean." Moved with pity, he stretched out his hand and touched him, and said to him, "I will; be clean." And immediately the leprosy left him, and he was made clean. And he sternly charged him, and sent him away at once, and said to him, "See that you say nothing to any one; but go, show yourself to the priest, and offer for your cleansing what Moses commanded, for a proof to the people." [45]But he went out and began to talk freely about

it, and to spread the news, so that Jesus could no longer openly enter a town, but was out in the country; and people came to him from every quarter.

CHAPTER 2

And when he returned to Capernaum after some days, it was reported that he was at home. And many were gathered together, so that there was no longer room for them, not even about the door; and he was preaching the word to them. And they came, bringing to him a paralytic carried by four men. And when they could not get near him because of the crowd, they removed the roof above him; and when they had made an opening, they let down the pallet on which the paralytic lay. 5And when Jesus saw their faith, he said to the paralytic, "My son, your sins are forgiven." Now some of the scribes were sitting there, questioning in their hearts, "Why does this man speak thus? It is blasphemy! Who can forgive sins but God alone?" And immediately Jesus, perceiving in his spirit that they thus questioned within themselves, said to them, "Why do you question thus in your hearts? Which is easier, to say to the paralytic, 'Your sins are forgiven,' or to say, 'Rise, take up your pallet and walk'? 10But that you may know that the Son of man has authority on earth to forgive sins"—he said to the paralytic— "I say to you, rise, take up your pallet and go home." And he rose, and immediately took up the pallet and went out before them all; so that they were all amazed and glorified God, saying, "We never saw anything like this!"

He went out again beside the sea; and all the crowd gathered about him, and he taught them. And as he passed on, he saw Levi the son of Alphaeus sitting at the tax office, and he said to him, "Follow me." And he rose and followed him.

[15]And as he sat at table in his house, many tax collectors and sinners were sitting with Jesus and his disciples; for there were many who followed him. And the scribes of the Pharisees, when they saw that he was eating with sinners and tax collectors, said to his disciples, "Why does he eat with tax collectors and sinners?" And when Jesus heard it, he said to them, "Those who are well have no need of a physician, but those who are sick; I came not to call the righteous, but sinners."

Now John's disciples and the Pharisees were fasting; and people came and said to him, "Why do John's disciples and the disciples of the Pharisees fast, but your disciples do not fast?" And Jesus said to them, "Can the wedding guests fast while the bridegroom is with them? As long as they have the bridegroom with them, they cannot fast. [20]The days will come, when the bridegroom is taken away from them, and then they will fast in that day. No one sews a piece of unshrunk cloth on an old garment; if he does, the patch tears away from it, the new from the old, and a worse tear is made. And no one puts new wine into old wineskins; if he does, the wine will burst the skins, and the wine is lost, and so are the skins; but new wine is for fresh skins."

One sabbath he was going through the grainfields; and as they made their way his disciples began to pluck heads of grain. And the Pharisees said to him, "Look, why are they doing what is not lawful on the sabbath?" [25]And he said to them, "Have you never read what David did, when he was in need and was hungry, he and those who were with him: how he entered the house of God, when Abiathar was high priest, and ate the bread of the Presence, which it is not lawful for any but the priests to eat, and also gave it to those who were with him?" And he said to them, "The sabbath was made for man, not man for the sabbath; so the Son of man is lord even of the sabbath."

CHAPTER 3

Again he entered the synagogue, and a man was there who had a withered hand. And they watched him, to see whether he would heal him on the sabbath, so that they might accuse him. And he said to the man who had the withered hand, "Come here." And he said to them, "Is it lawful on the sabbath to do good or to do harm, to save life or to kill?" But they were silent. [5]And he looked around at them with anger, grieved at their hardness of heart, and said to the man, "Stretch out your hand." He stretched it out, and his hand was restored. The Pharisees went out, and immediately held counsel with the Herodians against him, how to destroy him.

What's Happening Here?

From chapter 1, verse 14 to chapter 3, verse 6, Mark builds on the themes he presented in the introduction. He's concerned about the reaction of the crowd to Jesus, the calling of some of his disciples (though they don't act like his disciples here), and the growing opposition of the Jewish leaders to Jesus. And in the background of all these themes is the main point: Jesus begins very cautiously to demonstrate who he is, his own identity. He comes to an awareness of his own identity and he reveals that identity to the crowds gradually. He keeps his Messiahship a secret, mainly because the crowds wouldn't understand the kind of Messiah Jesus was. Mark develops his gospel in the same way, like a television mystery show which gradually unravels until the ending when everything becomes clear. We know then who did what and why. But until that time, it's a secret. The gospel of Mark deals with the "Messianic Secret."

If you want a two-line summary of what any gospel is about, just read Mark, chapter 1, verses 14 and 15. This is an editorial faith-comment of Mark. The scene is Galilee, away from Jerusalem, where according to Mark, Jesus did most of his work. Jerusalem is the center for Judaism, and since Mark is writing for Gentiles, he keeps Jesus out of that city until the Passion. The author is subtly telling the early Church that they don't have to turn to the Jerusalem Christian Church as the only or best community. Mark's summary of the Jesus message is simple: "Through Jesus, God is among us. Believe that and live accordingly."

Notice there's no reference to the birth or infancy of Jesus in Mark's gospel. For Mark the important feature of Jesus is his proclamation of the reign of God, and that proclamation begins with his public ministry.

This gospel episode recounted by Mark deals with discipleship. Jesus calls the "privileged" disciples first: Peter, James, and John. This is not just a passing casual meeting; it's an example of Jesus' power to create disciples. The impression here is that the disciples must give up their livelihood and abandon their families. But that's not really the point; rather, the idea is that discipleship entails great change. It's a question of priorities—what comes first. For a disciple the reign of God comes first. For Peter, before he followed Jesus, his job came first. After the death of Jesus, Peter significantly goes back to fishing. He goes back to putting his job first; he gives up his discipleship. Then when he believes in the Resurrection of Jesus, he once again puts his discipleship first. He becomes a "fisher of men." Jesus isn't opposed to fishing, nor should everyone leave their families. But to be a disciple, a Christian must put the reign of God first, regardless of his job or family situation.

The rest of chapter 1 could be called a typical day in the ministry of Jesus. This section explains the authority of Jesus, both in word and deed. He teaches in the synagogue and people are amazed. Mark doesn't tell us what he preaches, but as the gospel unfolds it becomes evident that the main message of Jesus is a declaration of who he is. It's a self-revelation—that's what he teaches in the first half of the gospel. And he does so in a veiled way. He taught in a way that was unusual, not like the scribes. He was not a "lower" teacher; he taught with power, the same power which overcame the evil forces in the temptation in the desert.

It's significant that the first miracle Mark recounts is an exorcism, that is, driving out a demon. Many miracles are described as exorcisms. Whether this means actual devil possession, or whether it's a psychotic person, isn't the real point. In either case, Jesus demonstrates his power over evil. The sickness, whatever its real nature, is a symbol of the power of destructive forces. Jesus faces that power head-on, and drives it away. He will continue to meet those forces in many ways throughout the gospel. The final evil he deals with is his own death. And in that struggle, as in all the rest, he triumphs— as long as there is some indication of faith on the part of the recipient of his power.

The evil spirit recognizes Jesus as a force for good, but the crowd doesn't see it. They are simply amazed by the curing and miss the message.

The story of Simon's mother-in-law provides some more insights into the message of Jesus. First of all, a few verses earlier Peter left his trade to follow Jesus. But with this incident recounted almost immediately, we see that a disciple need not abandon his family. Secondly, the setting here is the privacy of a home. The "privileged" disciples are there, and generally in those kinds of situations Jesus does something very special. The early Church viewed this episode as a preview of the coming resurrection of Jesus, and that's the way Mark tells it. Thirdly, this story indicates another dimension of discipleship— namely, service of others. When Jesus makes a disciple, that person immediately serves others, as did Peter's mother-in-law. Finally, we know from this account that Peter was married, as is probably the case with all the disciples except John.

As his hectic day comes to an end, Jesus is imposed upon by other people. His day is a long one; he is probably tired, but he continues his work. Mark presents it this way to show that Jesus did not restrict his teaching and his concern to only a few chosen people. He helped all who came to him. Once again, the demons recognize Jesus as a source of good, even as the Messiah, but the crowds still don't get the message.

The crowds are excited by this spectacular healer. It's like a sideshow. That's why Jesus leaves that town (although Simon wants him to stay and capitalize on his growing popularity) and goes to the desert to pray. In Mark's gospel, when Jesus prays it is a time of great stress connected with the true nature of his Messiahship. The crowds aren't reacting the way he wanted; they see his power, but don't hear his message. So Jesus leaves to think it all through and to pray about what he should do. He decides to move on to other places and try his luck there, the implication being that he was a little disappointed with this beginning of his ministry. Even Simon got it wrong.

The cure of a leper is significant because it indicates Jesus' power to save even those who were excluded from Israel by the law of Moses. Lepers were outcasts of society and could not participate in the social and religious life of Israel. Mark includes this cure in the story in order to demonstrate the extent of Jesus' ability to confront evil and surpass it. The man was sent back to the priest so that he could once again be accepted officially within Jewish society and religion. Typically he was asked to keep quiet about the cure—because Jesus was afraid the crowds would once again misinterpret the meaning of his power. The cured leper, of course, tells everyone about it. The early Church read this passage as an expression of their belief that those who are cleansed by Christ in Baptism must "proclaim" the good news.

Most of chapter 2 deals with controversy. The Pharisees, a powerful group of Jewish religious and political leaders, are afraid of Jesus. They judge him to be unfit for teaching and to be misleading the people. Their attempts to trap Jesus in a violation of the Law take up a good part of the gospel. They are scandalized by Jesus' conduct and words.

The story of the paralytic is a little confusing, because at one point, in verse 10, it seems that Jesus starts talking to a different audience. Probably Mark included this verse for the sake of the early Church, to spell out more clearly the meaning of the passage. In any case, the main message here is not difficult: Jesus claims the unusual power to forgive sins. The scribes and Pharisees object. Sin for them is a violation of the Law of Moses and only God can forgive sin and then only by fulfilling the requirements of Law for forgiveness of sin. Jesus shows them that the power he has in curing a paralytic, a sickness which again is a symbol of the presence of evil, is the same power he has in curing sin, another kind of sickness and another sign of the presence of evil. Jesus' battle against evil is total — nothing escapes his desire to confront those destructive forces.

A requirement for the cure, both of the physical sickness and of sin, is faith. The recipient must believe in Jesus — this curing is not magic. But the faith demanded here certainly is not faith in the divinity of Jesus. That belief can only be expected after the Resurrection; it was an important dimension for the early Christians. The faith expressed by the paralytic is probably a faith that Jesus could heal, that he was spokesman for God. Since the paralytic manifested that kind of faith, Jesus could release his healing word.

Characteristically, the people fail to see the miracle as a sign of Jesus' power to forgive sins. They marvel at the deed itself, without understanding the meaning of the deed.

The call of Levi is similar to the call of the other disciples, but Mark includes it here because it is another example of conflict between Jesus and the Pharisees. The Pharisees feel that Jesus is contaminated by "those terrible sinners." Jesus says he's there to help people, all people. The early Christians probably enjoyed this passage, because most of them were not scribes and Pharisees before they became Christians. The first Christians were, according to the scribes and Pharisees, sinners.

Mark follows immediately with another story that pits Jesus against the Pharisees. This time the topic is fasting, a practice the Pharisees are very insistent upon. Jesus is not opposed to fasting; he objects to the attitude which says that fasting automatically makes you a better person. Perhaps Jesus doesn't demand fasting of his followers because he wants to avoid the idea that fasting works automatically. Jesus looks for and encourages a personal faith response from people, not a particular practice. After that faith has been felt, then Christians can and should perform practices similar to fasting. But the faith commitment comes first, and during the life of Jesus, that kind of faith response has not yet been made by the disciples.

Mark also indicates that the reign of God is unique; it's brand new. It follows from the religious experience of Israel and the rest of the world, but it is decidedly different. It is a radical departure from man's previous religious experiences. Therefore, we can't force the reign of God into old patterns, old wineskins or a patched-up piece of cloth. It just doesn't work.

The controversy with the Pharisees grows. Jesus now challenges them on a very sensitive topic: the observance of the Sabbath laws. The Pharisees were strict observers of all the many regulations regarding the Sabbath, and they felt that their salvation depended on keeping those laws exactly. Jesus responds to their accusation by playing their own legal game and beats them on their own ground. Even David violated the law when circumstances demanded it. Law is not unimportant, but faith is more important. The Sabbath is not unimportant; but man is more important. This attitude was helpful to the early Christians because they had to decide to what extent they would follow the Jewish Sabbath regulations.

Jesus goes back to the synagogue where the Pharisees are bound to see and hear him. He was not afraid of them. He cures a man with a withered hand—once again on the Sabbath. The time is what is important, not the cure. Mark records the anger of Jesus; the other evangelists seem embarrassed to do so.

In chapter 3, verse 6, we see the conclusion to this section of the gospel. The opposition Jesus met from the Pharisees reaches its inevitable outcome: They plot to destroy him. The Pharisees joined with the Herodians. That's a very unusual alignment, since those two groups opposed each other on everything else. It's like liberal Democrats and conservative Republicans joining together, or even more dramatically, like the Black Panthers uniting with the Ku Klux Klan. In any case, Mark implies here that Jews of all kinds conspired to kill Jesus.

Where Did This Message Come From?

It might seem strange that Jesus was constantly telling people, especially those he just cured, to keep quiet about the cure. Mark emphasizes this aspect of the gospel. But both Mark and Jesus had a very good reason for presenting the message this way.

Jesus lived at a particular time, in a particular place. What the people at that time and place felt and thought was extremely important. The message Jesus wanted to deliver had to be offered in a language the people could understand. Jesus had to speak their language. And words have different meanings; sometimes the same word has different meanings for different people. Take the word "freedom," for example. For some people, freedom means doing whatever they want when they want to do it; for others, it means consideration of others and their needs; and for still others, it implies the making and the enforcing of good laws. Then there's the distinction between political freedom, social freedom, economic freedom, and personal, psychological freedom. Discussions on freedom can be confusing when it isn't clear what kind of freedom individuals are talking about.

Jesus was face-to-face with a similar language problem. The word causing the problem was "Messiah." The Jewish people at the time of Jesus were expecting a Messiah, as they had for many years. But the kind of Messiah they expected was a very specific brand. They wanted a Messiah who would lead them in a political revolt against the Romans who had conquered their country and were occupying it. The Jews felt that the Messiah would bring an easy life, full of wealth and control over the rest of the world. This Messiah would have armies and would be unbeatable since God would be with him. He would do spectacular things and eventually all the nations would bow to him and recognize him as the Messiah, the special messenger of God.

The kind of Messiah Jesus preached was a much different type of person. Jesus' Messiah would be humble and would have to suffer and die. The people couldn't understand that message.

Jesus tried to prepare the people for this message. He made constant references to Old Testament passages which indicated a suffering Messiah, but they didn't want to hear it. He pointed out that the Messiah would cure sicknesses and bring peace to man, but that idea fell on deaf ears also.

What Jesus wanted to do, as Mark develops it, was to gradually lead the people to understanding and accepting *his* kind of Messiah, a Messiah that is actually more accurate in terms of the Old Testament tradition. He knew however, that if he immediately announced that he was the long-awaited Messiah, the crowd would think of *their* kind of Messiah, not his kind. So, he attempted to get his meaning across slowly. That's why he told people to keep quiet about his cures; he knew they would misinterpret their real significance.

The word Messiah means "the anointed one." The Messiah was not necessarily the Son of God; he did not have to be divine. In fact, God-becoming-man was foreign to the Jewish way of thinking. For them, there was just one God; his name was Yahweh, and he had no equals. It took the Jews many centuries to come to that belief, but by the time of Jesus it was firmly entrenched in their religious lives. They couldn't conceive of more than one God, let alone of a man as God. That was blasphemy to them. So when they thought of the coming Messiah, they did not dream that the Messiah could also be God. Someone special, yes; but God, no!

It's a very difficult situation then for Jesus. He had to change their notion of Messiah, and he had to introduce them to the idea that the greatest thing God could do for man was to become man. Before his Resurrection, Jesus never did get his complete message across. He failed — until the Resurrection. And perhaps that was the only way in which he could truly succeed, by suffering and dying, a victim of the people's prejudices and inability to listen to his message, and a victim of everyone's involvement with evil.

Mark, in writing his gospel, was looking back into

the events of Jesus' life and interpreting those events in the light of his faith in the Resurrection. That belief colored his account; the gospel is not a history book in the sense most familiar to us. A good history book today will try to be objective; the author will attempt to keep his own feelings out of the text. He may not be able to do it completely, but he will have to try if he is to be accepted as a reliable historian. His task is to present the events as accurately as possible, just the way they happened and the reasons why they happened that way. Mark did not write that kind of history; Mark wrote about the early Christians and their faith in the Risen Lord. He *wants* to include their feelings and those things which he can't logically prove. His writing is more of a testimony than a modern history book.

And yet it is a true history, in the sense that people's feelings and beliefs are a definite and important part of the past. Mark didn't "make it all up"; he recorded past events plus the meaning of those events as felt and interpreted by a believing community. And that is history; Christians did believe that Jesus rose from the dead and therefore his life took on new meaning. In the light of this Resurrection faith, many things Jesus said and did finally made sense to the disciples. They didn't understand at the time, but they got the message later, and then knew what it was all about.

It's with this perspective—the history of Jesus as faith history—in mind that we are to read the gospel of Mark.

So What?

Our age has been described as a time of few commitments. It's a period when people hedge on things. Many delay making a choice of jobs until they are absolutely forced into it, and then they take the job only until they can find a better one, oftentimes meaning one that can make them more money. There's much discussion these days about personal commitments: How long should that commitment be? Trial marriages imply a temporary commitment. Our divorce courts give us ample evidence that many couples change their minds about each other. Our society is very mobile; people change their living quarters and neighborhood on the average of once every five years. Our methods of transportation are so fast that the whole world is rapidly becoming available to everyone. Television has introduced us to a great variety of events and styles of life. Ideas are everywhere: Last year's best-seller has to move over quickly for this year's major book.

Add all these developments together and we have quite an array of options. Which do we choose to follow for ourselves? It seems that a good number of people decide to try a little of this and a little of that. Try one approach for a few years, see where that leads you, and then perhaps try another approach. This may be either good or bad for an individual. We couldn't say unless we knew many other factors in the person's life. But one result does seem apparent: People have a tendency to avoid long-term, deeply-held commitments. Even parents who have specific responsibilities for their families sometimes give

the impression that they are not deeply committed to those responsibilities. They would much rather be doing something else, but they'll keep at it because they "have to." Once again, without judging whether this situation is always good or bad, it does raise a question about the possibility of deep and permanent commitments to anything or anyone.

This observation flows from the description of discipleship as presented in the gospel of Mark. Discipleship means some kind of commitment to the message and mission of the person of Jesus. Is discipleship possible in this hurry-up twentieth century? It's possible because it seems a number of people are doing it. Putting the reign of God first in whatever situation a person finds himself is a powerful challenge. But it can be done. What it would take would be a change in attitude and a decision to actively believe that, through Jesus, God is present to us, with his message of concern for others and gratitude for the life we live. Discipleship means sharing a vision of life; it means doing whatever a person can best do, and doing it for others in a spirit of genuine helpfulness and joy.

The cost of discipleship may be high; in the words of the song, Jesus "never promised us a rose garden." A disciple may face ridicule and rejection; he may have to suffer. And it will take a commitment, a risk. Can you do it? Do you want to do it? Why or why not?

Another aspect of this section in the gospel of Mark

concerned hypocrisy. Jesus associated with tax-collectors and "sinners." Tax-collectors were despised because they worked for the Romans and they quite frequently were involved in blackmail and extortion. Jesus was with these "outcasts" of society. The challenge for us today is obvious: do we dare to associate with the "outcasts" of our society? Who are those outcasts?

The impression is that people generally form their own group of friends and seldom pay much attention to other individuals or groups. Sometimes they then condemn the other groups because they are not like "my group." It's the old seesaw game: The other person has to be put-down so that I can be raised higher. "I'm better than the next guy because he's lower than me." This attitude is hypocritical, and it can be changed by doing what Jesus did: accept people as equals and friends. Marvelous things then happen.

To be a disciple implies a genuine commitment, avoiding hypocrisy. It also demands courage. To stand up for our convictions in the face of opposition is another mark of the disciple, as indicated in this section of Mark's gospel. The Pharisees tried to trap Jesus, and make him compromise his mission. They wanted him under their thumb, so they could control him. When they failed in their attempts to discredit him, they resorted to more drastic measures—plotting to kill him. But Jesus refused to compromise. He knew what was right, and he courageously stuck to his guns.

Do we share in that uncompromising courage to do what is right? Sometimes we have difficulty in determining what is the right thing to do in a particular situation. That difficulty is understandable; Jesus had to leave for the desert for a while to figure out what he should do next. He prayed over it and thought about it. But then he decided and carried out that decision. Determining what is right for a disciple may not be easy, and making decisions may be twice as hard. But we can make a few definite statements about the attitudes that are consistent with a true disciple of Jesus. Sometimes we simply need the courage to carry out those attitudes in our own situation.

Concern for other people is one of those attitudes. We might begin with our own families. Many teenagers are gradually becoming more independent. They are forming the ability to make their own decisions and insisting on their right to determine their own style of life. The influence of their parents is slowly slipping into the background. In this time of life when teenagers are still living at home, but when their real interests are no longer home-centered, conflicts arise between parents and teenagers. One mark of a teenage Christian would be his or her expressed concern for his or her parents as both parents and teenager try to work out this problem of dependence and independence. Show that concern in the many possible situations in which concern can help and heal; this approach doesn't mean that every one will agree on everything, but it does mean that concern for others is more important than agreement.

Oftentimes it seems that teenagers know how they can express that concern for their parents, but they are reluctant to do it because the courage to do it may be weak. They may be afraid of the opinions of their friends, or they may be afraid to listen attentively to their parents' position. It takes courage to be concerned about other people, and perhaps a great amount of courage to express that concern to the people we live with.

Commitment and courage—these two seeds lead to true discipleship. We may be committed and we may be courageous. More than likely most of us are a little committed and a little courageous. Those qualities can grow if we nourish them.

Parables Tell the Story

Mark 3:7—4:34

3:7

Jesus withdrew with his disciples to the sea, and a great multitude from Galilee followed; also from Judea and Jerusalem and Idumea and from beyond the Jordan and from about Tyre and Sidon a great multitude, hearing all that he did, came to him. And he told his disciples to have a boat ready for him because of the crowd, lest they should crush him; 10for he had healed many, so that all who had diseases pressed upon him to touch him. And whenever the unclean spirits beheld him, they fell down before him and cried out, "You are the Son of God." And he strictly ordered them not to make him known.

And he went up on the mountain, and called to him those whom he desired; and they came to him. And he appointed twelve, to be with him, and to be sent out to preach 15and have authority to cast out demons: Simon whom he surnamed Peter; James the son of Zebedee and John the brother of James, whom he surnamed Boanerges, that is, sons of thunder; Andrew, and Philip, and Bartholomew, and Matthew, and Thomas, and James the son of Alphaeus, and Thaddaeus, and Simon the Cananaean, and Judas Iscariot, who betrayed him.

Then he went home; 20and the crowd came together again, so that they could not even eat. And when his family heard it, they went out to seize him, for they said, "He is beside himself." And the scribes who came down from Jerusalem said, "He is possessed by Beelzebul, and by the prince of demons he casts out the demons." And he called them to him, and said to them in parables, "How can Satan cast out Satan? If a kingdom is divided against itself, that kingdom cannot stand. 25And if a house is divided against itself, that house will not be able to stand. And if Satan has risen up against himself and is divided, he cannot stand, but is coming to an end. But no one can enter a strong man's house and plunder his goods, unless he first binds the strong man; then indeed he may plunder his house.

"Truly, I say to you, all sins will be forgiven the sons of men, and whatever blasphemies they utter; but whoever blasphemes against the Holy Spirit never has forgiveness, but is guilty of an eternal sin" —[30]for they had said, "He has an unclean spirit."

And his mother and his brothers came; and standing outside they sent to him and called him. And a crowd was sitting about him; and they said to him, "Your mother and your brothers are outside, asking for you." And he replied, "Who are my mother and my brothers?" And looking around on those who sat about him, he said, "Here are my mother and my brothers! [35]Whoever does the will of God is my brother, and sister, and mother."

CHAPTER 4

Again he began to teach beside the sea. And a very large crowd gathered about him, so that he got into a boat and sat in it on the sea; and the whole crowd was beside the sea on the land. And he taught them many things in parables, and in his teaching he said to them: "Listen! A sower went out to sow. And as he sowed, some seed fell along the path, and the birds came and devoured it. [5]Other seed fell on rocky ground, where it had not much soil, and immediately it sprang up, since it had no depth of soil; and when the sun rose it was scorched, and since it had no root it withered away. Other seed fell among thorns and the thorns grew up and choked it, and it yielded no grain. And other seeds fell into good soil and brought forth grain, growing up and increasing and yielding thirtyfold and sixtyfold and a hundredfold." And he said, "He who has ears to hear, let him hear."

¹⁰And when he was alone, those who were about him with the twelve asked him concerning the parables. And he said to them, "To you has been given the secret of the kingdom of God, but for those outside everything is in parables; so that they may indeed see but not perceive, and may indeed hear but not understand; lest they should turn again, and be forgiven." And he said to them, "Do you not understand this parable? How then will you understand all the parables? The sower sows the word. ¹⁵And these are the ones along the path, where the word is sown; when they hear, Satan immediately comes and takes away the word which is sown in them. And these in like manner are the ones sown upon rocky ground, who, when they hear the word, immediately receive it with joy; and they have no root in themselves, but endure for a while; then, when tribulation or persecution arises on account of the word, immediately they fall away. And others are the ones sown among thorns; they are those who hear the word, but the cares of the world, and the delight in riches, and the desire for other things, enter in and choke the word, and it proves unfruitful. ²⁰But those that were sown upon the good soil are the ones who hear the word and accept it and bear fruit, thirtyfold and sixtyfold and a hundredfold."

And he said to them, "Is a lamp brought in to be put under

a bushel, or under a bed, and not on a stand? For there is nothing
hid, except to be made manifest; nor is anything secret, except
to come to light. If any man has ears to hear, let him hear."
And he said to them, "Take heed what you hear; the measure
you give will be the measure you get, and still more will
be given you. [25]For to him who has will more be given; and from
him who has not, even what he has will be taken away."

And he said, "The kingdom of God is as if a man should
scatter seed upon the ground, and should sleep and rise night
and day, and the seed should sprout and grow, he knows not
how. The earth produces of itself, first the blade, then the ear,
then the full grain in the ear. But when the grain is ripe, at once
he puts in the sickle, because the harvest has come."

[30]And he said, "With what can we compare the kingdom of
God, or what parable shall we use for it? It is like a grain of
mustard seed, which, when sown upon the ground, is the
smallest of all the seeds on earth; yet when it is sown it grows
up and becomes the greatest of all shrubs, and puts forth large
branches, so that the birds of the air can make nests in its
shade."

With many such parables he spoke the word to them, as
they were able to hear it; he did not speak to them without a
parable, but privately to his own disciples he explained everything.

What's Happening Here?

The disappointing reaction of the crowd to Jesus' preaching and healing leads him into phase two of his ministry. He decides to concentrate on forming a small group of special disciples, the hope being that with an intense training period and personal exposure to Jesus, they will finally understand his true message. The first part of this section (the rest of chapter 3 in the gospel) describes his attempts to pull away from the crowds, attempts which are not always successful. The second half of this passage (chapter 4:1-34) presents a number of parables, another device Jesus uses to point out various aspects of the reign of God.

The cities mentioned in verse 8 are not random choices; they are important cities where presumably early Christian communities developed. Mark, in other words, is complimenting those Christian communities by mentioning them.

In forming his small group of twelve, Jesus indicates his close connection with the Old Testament. The twelve are a symbolic continuation of the twelve tribes of Israel. These select disciples are to be "close to Jesus," to be his companions. A mark of apostleship then is this closeness to the Master; and in the early Church, after the Resurrection, it is precisely this constant companionship which provided these apostles with the base of their influence. St. Paul has to go to some length to prove his apostleship, because he did not experience this closeness in the same way the apostles mentioned here did. It is obvious from the text that Jesus wanted this group and made them "special." They even receive power to drive out "demons," that is, they participate in establishing the reign of God in a very dramatic way.

The names of the twelve are interesting and the listing is probably included here to demonstrate the diversity within the group. Jesus did not pick all the same kind of people; they were from different economic and social backgrounds (Peter the fisherman, Matthew the tax-collector) and even from different national backgrounds. Andrew, for example, is a good Greek name. Simon the Zealot was undoubtedly a political activist; the Zealot party was dedicated to the overthrow of the Romans, with violence if necessary. It's not surprising that the gospels give indications that this group didn't get along together too well. They argued among themselves about who was the best, and they disputed with Jesus and each other about the methods of preaching and what they should do next. The fact that Judas eventually betrayed Jesus indicates that this "disciple" could be disloyal not only to the Master but also to the other eleven men. The force of Jesus' personality must have been powerful in order to hold that group together for as long as he did.

The opposition to Jesus continues, and it seems to expand. Even his kinsmen join in condemning him. They conclude that he is insane, while the scribes claim that he is possessed by the devil. Both those accusations amount to the same thing, since insanity in those days was considered the work of the devil. It's to be expected therefore that Jesus would begin to feel lonely and disappointed; even his family participated in the opposition which eventually led to his death.

The response Jesus makes once again confounds his accusers. "How in the world can I be working for the devil, when I'm driving out devils? If you're going to condemn me for something, you're going to have to come up with something better than that!"

The next few verses are interesting because Jesus, who usually forgives sinners of just about everything, points to an "unforgivable sin." What is unforgivable is denying the power of God. If someone ascribes God's power to some other force, then that person can't be forgiven by God, since he doesn't even admit that power. But once a person admits that God has the power to forgive and asks for that forgiveness, then his mercy is present. The scribes had attributed Jesus' power to the devil, which is precisely the kind of sin Jesus refers to here.

Mark then includes the passage about the true family of Jesus, possibly because a few verses earlier, his blood relatives called him insane. The "brothers and sisters" of Jesus can easily be understood as his cousins, since that's one of the meanings of the original word. This episode does not indicate a lack of tenderness for relatives; it merely reminds us that the bond of brotherhood in the reign of God is greater than blood ties. At times discipleship makes demands which go farther than the demands even of a natural family.

Chapter 4 of Mark's gospel is confusing. Most of this section consists of a number of parables. But that's not the most confusing part; the problem comes in when we try to separate one parable from another. The three levels of the development of a gospel are very much in evidence in this passage: the first level of the earliest tradition, when the three parables were simply combined; the second level of the explanation of the parable of the sower which a later church community probably used in their instruction classes; and finally, the third level of Mark's personal comments which can be discerned particularly in verses 11 and 12.

Summarized, these 34 verses include the following: three parables, two sayings, the interpretation of a parable, a saying about the purpose of parables, an introduction, and a conclusion.

More than likely these parables came late in Jesus' public career. Mark uses them rather early in his gospel, because they deal with the nature of the reign of God in a veiled way. The stories are meant to encourage Jesus' followers; the reign is here, but it's going to take some time for it to be completed. The disciples are expecting Jesus to "take over" the world, but he runs into opposition. They need to be patient amid all the adversity. In the early Church many Christians expected the second coming of Jesus within the near future, but the second coming did not happen; so *they* needed the message of patience as well. The parables give assurance: Despite all the setbacks and delay in the final victory over the forces of evil, the reign is truly established.

The contrast in the parable of the sower is between the three types of unfruitful soil, and the good soil in which the seed grows. The lesson is obvious: the reign of God will surely come even though it may not appear so. We must wait for the seed in the fruitful soil to grow. But its eventual fruitfulness is guaranteed.

Mark then states very clearly that some people will not understand the parables, not because the stories themselves are that difficult, but because some people don't want to hear the message. Or perhaps they can't understand it, since their concept of the Messiah was so much different from Jesus' concept. In any case, the implication here is that a person who has faith will appreciate the richness of the parables, while an unbeliever will not. It is not so much that Jesus deliberately confused his message by using parables; rather he tried to gradually lead them into a deeper understanding of all of the ramifications of the reign of God. His *intention* in using these examples was to clarify his preaching. But the *result* all too often was to confuse the crowds because his message challenged them to change their way of thinking and acting, and many people didn't want to change — or couldn't change. They were deeply ingrained in their thought patterns, and the teaching of Jesus was too new for them.

At times however, the disciples asked him to explain what he meant. When asked he would give an answer. This approach is consistent with the second phase of his ministry; namely, to instruct his disciples more intensely than the crowds.

The interpretation of the parable of the sower in verses 13-20 is probably the result of religious instructions given by members of the early Christian Church. The style of language and the vocabulary leads us to this conclusion. For example, the term "the word" appears eight times in this short section, and that term was a technical phrase used by the early Church for the gospel message. Besides, this interpretation concentrates on the different types of unfruitful soil which wasn't the main point of the original parable. It seems that this expansion of the sower story is geared towards encouraging perseverance in times of temptation and persecution.

In verses 21-25 Mark repeats himself. He stresses again the need to be ready and willing to hear the word of God. This idea was expressed earlier in this chapter, and apparently Mark felt it was so important that he states it again. To hear the message of Jesus a person must "open" himself, must prepare himself, and must dispose himself to receive the message. It does not happen automatically; the individual must make some effort himself.

The parable of the seed is similar to the story of the sower. Here the emphasis is on the inactivity of the farmer after he sows the seed. Once planted in good soil the seed will grow and the harvest will come. In other words, the fulfillment of the reign of God will surely come, since Jesus has already planted the seed.

Mark immediately adds a third parable related to planting. This time the reference is to the mustard seed. This seed is called the smallest of all the seeds, yet it really isn't the smallest. But the size of the seed isn't the real point. The main idea is to draw a contrast between seemingly insignificant beginnings and the final outcome: what starts small will grow to amazing proportions. The good news from Jesus will spread throughout the world until it reaches fulfillment. This one person living in this tiny land ushers in a worldwide revolution.

The conclusion of this section on parables re-emphasizes the intention and the results of Jesus' use of parables. Mark reminds us again that the crowds didn't understand Jesus, even when he tried to spell it out in simple story form. Consequently, Jesus was forced to turn more and more to his disciples, hoping that with his fuller explanations they at least would know what he was saying.

Where Did This Message Come From?

The reign of God is like an algebra course. A student enters the class in September, and the teacher introduces him to the textbook and gives him an outline of what to expect in the course. Other students are there. As time goes on, some students will not take algebra seriously and will not understand. Others will try to understand, but will be distracted by outside interests, and these students too will miss much of the meaning of algebra. Other pupils will pay attention, but because they have not been prepared adequately in previous mathematics courses, they will find the subject too difficult and will not learn the material. But there will be some students who listen to the teacher, study the material, do what is expected of them, and will learn to understand algebra.

This example from a class is an attempt at a modern parable. Parables were teaching devices used by Jesus to explain his message. He referred to life situations familiar to his audience. The previous example of a modern parable tried to demonstrate the same idea the parable of the sower tried to get across: Some students will surely learn algebra just like some seed will surely grow in good soil. By the same token, the reign of God has come in Jesus, even though viewed from some angles, it doesn't seem like it. In the same way some students may flunk the algebra course, others may barely pass, but some will do well.

We need to make a distinction at this point, a distinction between a parable and an allegory. Both are figures of speech involving the telling of a story. But a parable and an allegory have important differences as well.

First, what is a *parable*? The word "parable" comes from the Greek, and it means the "placing of things side by side for the sake of comparison." In a parable a story is told, and although the story may be fiction, it is still true to life. This feature, this true-to-lifeness, distinguishes a parable from a fable.

Then what is an *allegory*? In an allegory, each detail and character of the story is significant, oftentimes having a hidden meaning. Allegories tend to portray more abstract truth than a parable.

The important thing to remember about the distinction between an allegory and a parable is this: In a parable the most significant idea is the lesson of the whole story; the details serve only to bring out the main point. In any allegory, however, all the aspects of the story, each detail, has an important meaning. Sometimes, in a story which is basically a parable, there may be some allegorical features as well. In other words, in a story with one main point (parable) some of the characters or details may have a significance of their own (allegory).

This distinction is needed because Jesus told stories. If these stories were parables, we have to interpret them one way; if they are allegories, we have to interpret them differently, trying to discover the meaning of each detail. Some people, for example, have explained the story of the Good Samaritan as an allegory. They identify the "man who went down to Jericho" as Adam; Jerusalem means man in the garden of Eden; Jericho refers to man's mortality; the Samaritan is Christ; the inn is the Church; the innkeeper is St. Paul. If, on the other hand, we understand the story of the Good Samaritan as a parable, there is no need to identify and name all the aspects of the story.

Most Scripture scholars today would say that the stories of Jesus are basically parables, with some allegorical features mixed in occasionally. In chapter 4 of Mark's gospel, we read the parable of the sower. In verses 1-9, we find an example of a true parable, a story that has one main point. But in verses 13-20, we discover what appears to be an allegorical interpretation of the original story. More than likely, this allegorical interpretation was developed by the primitive Christian Church and not by Jesus himself.

Jesus was a good teacher in his use of parables. His illustrations were from daily life and caught the attention of his listeners. They could understand his message better, but at times he tossed in an unusual ending, a novel twist, that challenged his listeners to reflect on the main point. A case in point is the story of the woman who finds one small coin and rejoices exceedingly, over-rejoices it seems, just because she found one little coin. That technique was used to make people think.

Jesus referred often in his stories to rural Galilean life, to outdoor scenes of farming and shepherding. This approach, while it was perfect for the people of Jesus' time and locality, provides a difficulty for the modern reader, even for twentieth century farmers, since the farming techniques are so much different today. It almost seems that in order to understand the parables in all their meaning, a modern reader needs considerable information about the culture and habits of people living in Galilee during the first century.

The parables of Jesus are not just cute, clever stories to inspire people. Many of them express his main purpose; namely, to proclaim the presence of the reign of God. As such, they are an integral part of his mission and imply a vigorous assault made by God against the forces of evil. The parables in chapter 4 of Mark's gospel were an explanation and an apology for the slowness and "insignificant" results of Jesus' own ministry in Galilee. And yet, they describe the reality of Jesus' power and give assurance of his final, complete victory.

So What?

Everyone has needs. They come in many areas of life, sometimes they are easily identified and sometimes they are cleverly disguised and hard to point out. We obviously have a need for food, water and air. Almost as obvious, but not always as easily attained, is our need for love and acceptance. Some psychologists have listed up to one hundred and forty different needs the human being seeks to fulfill. Most of the time we are not conscious of these desires, nor of the techniques we use to satisfy them. But most people would admit that they are operating

within us, helping to determine our style of life and our patterns of behavior.

We live today in what has been described as the "Now Generation." The implication is that we are to enjoy the present moment, taking advantage of the many opportunities for pleasure offered to us by our society. "Don't worry about the past, and the future will take care of itself. Concentrate on today!"

This invitation to get the most out of the present moment certainly has a number of advantages. It can make us more aware of what's going on around us, and it can open the door to more occasions for joyful experiences. It could encourage us to leave our past "hang-ups" behind us, and in doing so, lead us to greater personal freedom. The present moment, whatever it may be, has much to offer us.

And yet there may be a problem. We may begin to expect our needs to be satisfied immediately, in the present. And if those needs are not fulfilled now, we may experience undue frustration. We may lose an important perspective: The fact that today leads into tomorrow. Some of our needs are lifelong, and to fulfill them adequately takes a long time. But what we do today, how we face and react to those needs now, can contribute to the eventual, happy satisfaction of those legitimate desires. We may have to deal with some of those needs a little bit at a time.

Perhaps an example of this gradual fulfillment of our desires is our need for love. We need to love and be loved throughout our lives. As a child we should experience love as parental care for us; as adolescents we begin to learn the demands love makes on us; as adults we should assume more and more love-responsibilities; as old folks we could rest in the assurance and semi-completion of our loving and being loved. In other words, there are various stages in our love life, one hopefully leading to the other. To expect all of them at the same time seems unrealistic, if not downright unhealthy. But living one stage as best we can lays a solid foundation for a happy living of the next stage. It's a progression.

If we are too impatient, not realizing our future needs as well as our present needs for love, we run the risk of expecting too much from today and not enough from tomorrow. Perhaps it's this lack of awareness, this failure to face the future, which leads some people to enter an unwise marriage. Perhaps it's this same impatience which causes a student to neglect his studies with the explanation that his courses don't do much for him. The student reacts to his conscious and unconscious needs of today and refuses to consider his life situation five, ten, and even twenty years from now. Patience is an important factor in life.

The parables in the fourth chapter of Mark's gospel describe this same factor of patience. The establishment of the reign of God will not be completed soon. To expect it now would lead to a particular style of life, a more patient style which would encourage the Christian to actively participate in bringing about the full flowering of the reign. It's this kind of patience that the parables tried to inspire in believers, and it's this kind of active patience which can motivate Christians today.

There have been many changes in almost all Christian Churches in the past ten years. Most of those changes have been twofold; on the one hand, there's the desire to make the churches more adaptable to the twentieth century, to speak the language of modern man, to eliminate some of the trappings of the Middle Ages. On the other hand, there's the similar desire to make the churches more clearly reflective of the basic message of the gospels, to reexpress the simplicity, the comfort, and the challenge of Jesus; to reformulate the Christian belief in the spirit of the gospel. It's this twofold thrust which has inspired the many changes our churches have experienced.

And of course, there are those people who want and expect these changes to take place faster, those who want them to take place slower, and those who don't want them at all. This division in the Church can at times be healthy, and can at times be destructive. In either case, it seems necessary to recall the message of those parables: The reign of God will surely come, be patient amid all the setbacks, but continue to work for the fulfillment of that reign.

We need a combination of patience in which we look hopefully to the future, and of commitment by which we contribute to that future.

CHAPTER FOUR

Make Me a Miracle

Mark 4:35—6:6

4:35

On that day, when evening had come, he said to them, "Let us go across to the other side." And leaving the crowd, they took him with them in the boat, just as he was. And other boats were with him. And a great storm of wind arose, and the waves beat into the boat, so that the boat was already filling. But he was in the stern, asleep on the cushion; and they woke him and said to him, "Teacher, do you not care if we perish?" And he awoke and rebuked the wind, and said to the sea, "Peace! Be still!" And the wind ceased, and there was a great calm. [40]He said to them, "Why are you afraid? Have you no faith?" And they were filled with awe, and said to one another, "Who is this, that even wind and sea obey him?"

CHAPTER 5

They came to the other side of the sea, to the country of the Gerasenes. And when he had come out of the boat, there met him out of the tombs a man with an unclean spirit, who lived among the tombs; and no one could bind him any more, even with a chain; for he had often been bound with fetters and chains, but the chains he wrenched apart, and the fetters he broke in pieces; and no one had the strength to subdue him. [5]Night and day among the tombs and on the mountains he was always crying out, and bruising himself with stones. And when he saw Jesus from afar, he ran and worshiped him; and crying out with a loud voice, he said, "What have you to do with me, Jesus, Son of the Most High God? I adjure you by God, do not torment me." For he had said to him, "Come out of the man, you unclean spirit!" And Jesus asked him, "What is your name?" He replied, "My name is Legion; for we are many."

[10]And he begged him eagerly not to send them out of the country. Now a great herd of swine was feeding there on the hillside; and they begged him, "Send us to the swine, let us enter them." So he gave them leave. And the unclean spirits came out, and entered swine; and the herd, numbering about two thousand, rushed down the steep bank into the sea, and were drowned in the sea.

The herdsmen fled, and told it in the city and in the country. And people came to see what it was that had happened. [15]And they came to Jesus, and saw the demoniac sitting there, clothed and in his right mind, the man who had had the legion; and they were afraid. And those who had seen it told what had happened to the demoniac and to the swine. And they began to beg Jesus to depart from their neighborhood. And as he was getting into the boat, the man who had been possessed with demons begged him that he might be with him. But he refused, and said to him, "Go home to your friends, and tell them how much the Lord has done for you, and how he has had mercy on you." [20]And he went away and began to proclaim in the Decapolis how much Jesus had done for him; and all men marveled.

And when Jesus had crossed again in the boat to the other side, a great crowd gathered about him; and he was beside the sea. Then came one of the rulers of the synagogue, Jairus by name; and seeing him, he fell at his feet, and besought him, saying, "My little daughter is at the point of death. Come and lay your hands on her, so that she may be made well, and live." And he went with him.

And a great crowd followed him and thronged about him.
²⁵And there was a woman who had had a flow of blood for
twelve years, and who had suffered much under many phy-
sicians, and had spent all that she had, and was no better but
rather grew worse. She had heard the reports about Jesus, and
came up behind him in the crowd and touched his garment.
For she said, "If I touch even his garments, I shall be made
well." And immediately the hemorrhage ceased; and she felt in
her body that she was healed of her disease. ³⁰And Jesus; perceiving in himself that power had gone forth from him, immediately turned about in the crowd, and said, "Who touched
my garments?" And his disciples said to him, "You see the
crowd pressing around you, and yet you say, 'Who touched
me?'" And he looked around to see who had done it. But the
woman, knowing what had been done to her, came in fear and
trembling and fell down before him, and told him the whole
truth. And he said to her, "Daughter, your faith has made
you well; go in peace, and be healed of your disease."

³⁵While he was still speaking, there came from the ruler's
house some who said, "Your daughter is dead. Why trouble
the Teacher any further?" But ignoring what they said, Jesus
said to the ruler of the synagogue, "Do not fear, only believe."
And he allowed no one to follow him except Peter and James
and John the brother of James. When they came to the house
of the ruler of the synagogue, he saw a tumult, and people
weeping and wailing loudly. And when he had entered, he said
to them, "Why do you make a tumult and weep? The child is
not dead but sleeping." ⁴⁰And they laughed at him. But he put
them all outside, and took the child's father and mother and
those who were with him, and went in where the child was.

Taking her by the hand he said to her, "Talitha cumi"; which means, "Little girl, I say to you, arise." And immediately the girl got up and walked (she was twelve years of age), and immediately they were overcome with amazement. And he strictly charged them that no one should know this, and told them to give her something to eat.

CHAPTER 6

He went away from there and came to his own country; and his disciples followed him. And on the sabbath he began to teach in the synagogue; and many who heard him were astonished, saying, "Where did this man get all this? What is the wisdom given to him? What mighty works are wrought by his hands! Is not this the carpenter, the son of Mary and brother of James and Joses and Judas and Simon, and are not his sisters here with us?" And they took offense at him. And Jesus said to them, "A prophet is not without honor, except in his own country, and among his own kin, and in his own house." [5]And he could do no mighty work there, except that he laid his hands upon a few sick people and healed them. And he marveled because of their unbelief.

And he went about the villages teaching.

What's Happening Here?

Mark follows his presentation of three parables with an account containing three miracles, each performed for the benefit of the disciples. The crowds are still in the picture, but they continue to take a secondary place. A few chapters later in the gospel they will disappear almost completely, only to reappear during the Passion.

The first miracle is generally considered to be a personal recollection of the apostle Peter. But the episode is so reworked by the early Church that it is almost impossible to separate the actual event from the interpretation of the event by that primitive Christian community. The Church turned to this miracle for consolation, because the term "boat" has long been a symbol of the Church. There's a strong emphasis here on the storm and the need for faith, and so this incident becomes a lesson in discipleship under stress. The final question in this account, "Who can this be that the wind and sea obey him?" is significant in a number of ways. First, it continues the theme of searching for the true identity of Jesus: the Messianic secret is gradually being revealed in the actions of Jesus. Secondly, the verb "obey" is deliberately put into the present tense, indicating that the power of Jesus is still operative in the Church.

In this miracle, Jesus is called "Master" or "Teacher." Throughout the gospel of Mark this title is used in catechetical settings, episodes used by the first century Church to explain various aspects of Christianity. Employed here, it helps establish the fact that this miracle account was developed and reorganized to fit the purposes of the early Church.

Another implication of this miracle comes to light when the reader recalls the Old Testament imagery related to the sea. God's work in creation is described in the first book of Genesis as a conquest of the sea. For many religions in the Middle East the sea is the location of the evil gods. In the history of Israel, the sea almost always refers to the Reed Sea, the body of water the Israelites crossed when escaping from the Egyptians. That crossing, that Exodus, was the central event in the history of the Jews, and it was accomplished by the power of Yahweh. In this gospel miracle then, the same power is at work. Jesus shows the same mastery over the sea, and as such there is an implied statement about Jesus' equality with Yahweh.

Jesus condemns the disciples for their lack of faith. This judgment seems to be quite strong if we take it literally; that is, if Jesus made that condemnation before his Resurrection. More than likely, this judgment comes from Mark himself, as he remembers the disciples' loss of faith at Jesus' death.

The second miracle is hard to explain because of the connection between the swine and the maniac. One possible interpretation of this aspect of the story is that evil is self-destructive; that is, left to itself evil will destroy itself. Evil needs to fight against good, needs a foothold in good. Without that foothold, evil can't exist.

What may be even more significant than the miracle itself is its location, where it takes place. The territory of the Gerasene is outside of Israel. The maniac is a Gentile, and according to acceptable social customs among the Jews of Jesus' time, association with Gentiles was strongly discouraged. As a result, this account shows how Jesus won acceptance in a foreign land. Jesus confronted the power of the demons and defeated evil again, this time the result being an interest in Jesus by people outside Judaism. This theme of concern for Gentiles was certainly consoling for those Christians who were not previously Jewish.

Jesus is pictured as overpowering the adversary by learning his name. To know someone's name was to have influence over him. For us, a name is generally arbitrary. We could have any first name and still be the same person; it wouldn't make much difference. In Biblical times and in Hebrew thought-patterns, a name and a person were much more closely connected. In a sense, the name was the person; it did more than just point to the person. Since Jesus here learns the name of the demon, he has mastery over him. The name "legion," by the way, originally meant "soldier" and not "many." Someone translating the text apparently got the two mixed up.

Jesus does not allow the cured man to accompany him. It's hard to say why, but the important aspect of this part of the story is that Jesus does not appeal to the "Messianic Secret." Rather he tells the man to proclaim what has happened to him. Perhaps this command is due to the fact that the man is not a Jew and therefore does not entertain any false expectations of the coming Messiah. He can therefore simply proclaim what has happened and not draw any erroneous conclusions.

The third miracle is actually a combination of two different stories. The one concerns the daughter of Jairus, an influential man from the Jewish synagogue, and the second revolves around the woman suffering from a hemorrhage. Mark combines them, probably because of their similarity.

The confidence that Jairus exhibits is a distinct contrast to the distrust and hostility of the scribes. He expresses his belief that Jesus can do something for his daughter, and whenever Jesus meets that kind of recognition he offers to help. But the main purpose for including this episode in the gospel is to make a commentary on death. The raising of the daughter is a preview of Jesus' own resurrection; this is a key miracle for Mark, because miracles symbolize the passage from death to life. In this story Jesus confronts death directly and overcomes it; death is considered a major result of the forces of evil. Jesus does battle with evil in many ways, but none so directly as when he faces death, his own or others'.

The woman with the hemorrhage suffers not only from a physical ailment that has caused her many years of affliction, but also because she is considered "unclean" according to Jewish ceremonial law. To say the least, it was a grave inconvenience to her. It almost seems that the power of Jesus works like magic in this instance, but Mark immediately corrects that possible interpretation by the woman's admission of her "touching" his cloak. Jesus then says very clearly that her faith was a necessary disposition for the cure to take place. "Touching" Jesus generally means more than a physical laying on of hands; it likewise implies a "touching" of the person or the spirit of Jesus.

This section of the gospel closes with another and more extensive account of the rejection of Jesus. Previously, in Chapter 3, verse 6, the Pharisees and the Herodians began to plot against him. Here Jesus is condemned by his townspeople. While his popularity spreads, he likewise gains more enemies. Nazareth is the presumed place of this rejection, but in the context of the whole gospel this negative reaction is a foreshadowing of the final rejection in which all the people concur. It's interesting to note that Jesus teaches in Nazareth, but the crowd's response here is almost the exact opposite of their response in chapter 1, verses 21-27. There he found enthusiasm; here he runs into skepticism leading to explicit disbelief. These people want to know "Who is this man?" It's a good question, the basic question in terms of Mark's gospel. This group, however, does not ask the question honestly; they ask it in order to put Jesus down since they resent him. Because their attitude was so cynical and unbelieving, he could work no miracle there. This verse provides us with a clear example of the necessity for faith before Jesus can help an individual. Mark adds immediately, however, that not all the people rejected Jesus, and he could help those who accepted him.

This incident brings to a tragic end his ministry in Galilee and previews his coming complete rejection by the whole nation. After this episode, Jesus is determined more than ever to concentrate his efforts on the select twelve disciples; they begin to take a more active role in proclaiming the presence of the reign of God.

Where Did This Message Come From?

There are volumes of books, even complete libraries, dealing with the nature and the use of miracles. Some authors deny the possibility of any miracles; others claim that many events are miraculous. The authors don't agree on their definition of a miracle, and they dispute the purpose of the miraculous. Arguments about the formation of the Biblical accounts of miracles range from the position which maintains that the early Church made them all up in order to make Jesus look powerful, to the position which insists that Jesus performed the miracles exactly as recorded in the gospels. Other writers admit the basic accuracy of the Biblical record, but deny the present possibility of miracles. Others, of course, expect miracles in our day. Then again, there are those authors who think that although God *could* work miracles anytime he wanted to, he in fact *doesn't* act that way. To study all these theories is the task of the scholar, and most people have neither the inclination for such study, nor the time and perhaps not the ability to undertake such a job.

The "man in the street" probably has an opinion about miracles, simply because most people have been exposed to some kind of miracle story. Generally, it seems that the "common man" has a number of questions about the nature of the miraculous, questions that are basically unanswered, and yet he decides to either accept miracles or reject them, and he doesn't think about them very much. Other concerns occupy his interests.

To understand the gospel of Mark, however, we have to consider the question of miracles. To eliminate the miracle stories or to relegate them to fantasyland, to an area of relative unimportance, would be to cut a large portion out of the gospel. Those accounts are there— all over the place. They demand some kind of response.

One of the problems related to biblical miracles is that we have gradually learned to take them out of context. We have isolated the accounts of miracles, using them as weapons in our arguments to prove the divinity of Jesus. This approach is unfortunate, not because it is false in itself, but because it emphasizes an aspect of miracles which is not primary in the Scriptures. The gospels take the miraculous for granted; they do not try to "prove" the possibility of miracles. The gospels are concerned with *how* Jesus used miracles and what they meant to the evangelist. It's a very different approach, and these two different approaches have significant and diverse influences when it comes to interpreting the gospel miracles.

In clarifying these two differing approaches, it is helpful to turn to a definition of miracles as formulated by St. Thomas Aquinas. Thomas said that a miracle is an "action which surpassed the power of all nature." That formulation, or a similar one, is the generally accepted description of a miracle; it's an action which goes beyond the laws of nature.

Without quarreling with that definition, it is legitimate to point out that the biblical writers thought of miracles in very different terms. The Bible does not view nature as a closed system of laws; a clear distinction between natural and supernatural cannot be found in Scripture. Rather the "natural" and the "supernatural" are so joined together, are so blurred, that a separation of the two becomes impossible and artificial. According to the Bible, the workings of "nature," of "normal" events (like a flood or an invasion by an enemy army), are attributed directly to God. In other words, sometimes the Bible includes as equally miraculous those acts which can be explained on the "natural" level. Therefore, the Bible includes events which St. Thomas could not accept as miraculous, even though the Scripture unashamedly refers to them as miracles.

In the Old Testament, the Jews viewed the Exodus as their principle miracle. This great event could be explained as the result of very natural causes; some slaves made good their escape from their owners. This kind of escape happened frequently in the history of man. But for the Jews this particular attainment of freedom was interpreted with faith, and therefore the whole episode was accepted as a miraculous action of God. With that in mind, Jewish storytellers surrounded the historical event with awe-inspiring details (the ten plagues, the crossing of the Reed Sea). The main point here is that the Jewish escape was a miracle, but not necessarily what we might technically call "supernatural." Their God was with them, working for them, but they saw his presence and his power *within* ordinary, "natural" events. This is not to deny possible, extra-ordinary religious experiences; it is simply to say that from a biblical point of view the people did not "wait around" for the "supernatural" experiences before they believed in the presence of God.

It might be helpful also to point out that the word "miracle" does not actually appear in the New Testament. The English translation may be a little misleading here. The English word "miracle" comes from the Latin word "miraculum" which means "something to be wondered at." But the gospels were not written originally in Latin; they were written in Greek and Hebrew, with Aramaic having a very strong influence as well. The significance of this language reminder is that translations from one language to another sometimes lose the flavor of the original writing. In the case of the word "miracle," which in English denotes an element of the marvelous, we find the biblical text referring not to the marvelous aspect of the concept, but rather to the sign aspect. Put another way, we discover that the scriptural reference to what we translate as "miracle" means in the original Hebrew or Greek a "symbolic sign" or an "act of power." The Bible therefore does not give real emphasis to the marvelous character of a "miracle"; in fact, it need not refer to anything marvelous. Miracle in the biblical sense refers to any action or event which is a sign of God's presence or any act of power reflecting that presence.

These reflections are not just playing with words; they are distinctions needed in order to understand what Mark meant when he wrote about the miracles of Jesus. We make a mistake when we use our definition of miracle as spelled out by St. Thomas Aquinas and assume that the word meant exactly the same thing for Mark. To summarize the difference, and perhaps run the risk of oversimplifying, we might say that the common understanding of miracle (as with St. Thomas) means an "exceptionally marvelous happening," whereas for Mark it meant "a symbolic act." Those two descriptions are not absolutely opposed, but they do express a different approach.

According to many Scripture scholars there are two basic types of miracle narratives. The first are the *pronouncement miracle stories* and the second are *miracle stories proper*. A pronouncement miracle story is a story in which the important feature is a saying or teaching of Jesus. The miracle is part of the story in the sense that it emphasizes the point of the narrative; the miracle is recounted primarily for the sake of the pronouncement.

We saw a good example of that kind of miracle in chapter 3, verses 1-6, in Mark. There Jesus is talking about his power to forgive sins, which is his main point. Then the paralytic is lowered through the roof and Jesus cures him. The focus of the story is not on the cure itself; it centers rather on the message of forgiveness. Jesus says that he has power to forgive just as he has power to cure. This is a pronouncement miracle story.

The second type of miracle accounts are those in which the miracle itself is the center of interest. Many of the healing miracles fit into this category as well as the nature miracles (e.g., calming the sea). These miracle stories seem to have a fixed format. They begin with a *setting*, a description of the illness of the sick person with a comment about previous failures at healing. Oftentimes the setting includes an expression of doubt or scorn by onlookers, the implication being that Jesus can't help this sick person. But there's always someone, the stricken person himself or relatives, who gives voice to his belief that Jesus does have God's healing power available to him. After the setting, the *cure itself* takes place. Usually Jesus uses a simple word or a touch or spittle in these stories, and the effect is immediate. The *result* follows the cure; often the reality of the cure is attested to by the patient, and most of the time the crowd's response is one of amazement and wonder. The crowds are supposed to ask themselves, Who is this man who has such power? Too often however, they don't get beyond their own amazement.

Most miracle stories will have this basic structure.

This same structure does not mean that each miracle episode is expressing the same specific point. In the pronouncement stories it's relatively easy to get the main point of the passage. In the miracle stories proper, it can usually be said that Jesus is demonstrating the arrival of the reign of God through himself. In any case, a safe conclusion would be to say that the miracles as recorded in the gospel of Mark are of secondary importance to the message of Mark. It's that message and that mission of Jesus which is the primary theme and most emphatic aspect of the gospel. The miracles are part of that message and factors in that mission, but they do not stand alone. In a sense, they are visual aids used by Jesus and probably expanded by the early Church and Mark, used in order to help explain the main thrust of the message of Jesus. As such, the miracles are not just "added on" to prove the importance of the message; they are rather an integral part of the revelation since they demonstrate the power of Jesus' actions. They are a vehicle of the message, and they are a weapon in Jesus' struggle with the forces of evil. To eliminate the miracles from the gospels would be to eliminate a necessary part of the basic message of Jesus. Mark couldn't tell the complete story without them. Neither can we.

So What?

A poet once said that a person who loses his sense of wonder at the little things in our world will miss the big things as well. It's not just a question of practice.

It's more a question of sensitivity towards the beauty in the world around us, whether it be a flower, a sunset, the Grand Canyon, or a person.

Looking for beauty in the people and events around us may be a luxury many of us don't engage in. We can often be tied down to the routine happenings of our lives: We take for granted the people we're most familiar with; we pass by our neighborhoods so many times, we don't see them any more; we look at the sky occasionally and move right on without a pause; we are hypnotized by television and don't see the view outside our window. If we live in a crowded city, we are often forced to miss the beauty of nature because of the buildings, the traffic, and the smog. Frequently we also miss the beauty of the people on the streets and in our neighborhood, probably because we concentrate on their plainness rather than their uniqueness, and on their "coolness" rather than their warmth. Much in life can go right by us if we don't make the effort to look for it.

The discussion about biblical miracles may help us recapture some of the sense of wonder and excitement we had as little children. We were curious about many things when we were children; we asked many questions; we were thrilled by little things. We grew up and we probably lost much of the enthusiasm as we experienced the responsibilities of life and the familiarity of our surroundings. We cannot return to childishness, nor to a time when there were no responsibilities. But we can be childlike in some of the aspects of our response to life

regardless of our age. And it may be this factor of child-like wonder which the gospel miracles may present to us.

The miracle stories in Mark's gospel are signs of the presence of God, and as we saw in the previous section, they need not be the extraordinary happenings. They may be "normal" events viewed from a faith perspective. They are expressions of a Christian belief that our God is with us, active in our world even within those ordinary events we are so familiar with. Wherever there is good and beauty and truth, there is God. To be sensitive to the truth, the beauty, and the good in our world and in people is, for the Christian, to be sensitive to the miracle of the continuing presence of God made particularly manifest through Jesus of Nazareth.

It is the miracle of the ordinary which most of us have to deal with. The "marvelous" happening, though possible, is usually rare for the majority of people. Even the sacraments, special signs of the presence of God and in that sense also miracles, are ordinary in that we can witness or participate in them often. Most of us are "doomed" to the supposed humdrum life of ordinary people trying to make the best of things. And that is precisely our fate unless we seek the miracle of the ordinary, the exciting message *behind* and *within* the familiar events and people around us.

What is a miracle? Where is one? Just look around you and within you, and you may find that miracle, that sign that God has not forgotten us. Of course as in any miracle at any time, to see it, to experience it, takes a degree of faith. Without that faith, there is no miracle and probably no mystery; there are only problems to be solved and a world to be put together as best we can. The gospels invite us to solve problems and work on the world, but they also offer us a belief in the miraculous activity of a God who continually manifests himself to us, most often in very ordinary ways.

CHAPTER FIVE

Food For All

Mark 6:7—7:37

6:7

And he called to him the twelve, and began to send them out two by two, and gave them authority over the unclean spirits. He charged them to take nothing for their journey except a staff; no bread, no bag, no money in their belts; but to wear sandals and not put on two tunics. ¹⁰And he said to them, "Where you enter a house, stay there until you leave the place. And if any place will not receive you and they refuse to hear you, when you leave, shake off the dust that is on your feet for a testimony against them." So they went out and preached that men should repent. And they cast out many demons, and anointed with oil many that were sick and healed them.

King Herod heard of it; for Jesus' name had become known. Some said, "John the baptizer has been raised from the dead; that is why these powers are at work in him." ¹⁵But others said, "It is Elijah." And others said, "It is a prophet, like one of the prophets of old." But when Herod heard of it he said, "John, whom I beheaded, has been raised." For Herod had sent and seized John, and bound him in prison for the sake of Herodias, his brother Philip's wife; because he had married her. For John said to Herod, "It is not lawful for you to have your brother's wife." And Herodias had a grudge against him, and wanted to kill him. But she could not, ²⁰for Herod feared John, knowing that he was a righteous and holy man, and kept him safe. When he heard him, he was much perplexed; and yet he heard him gladly. But an opportunity came when Herod on his birthday gave a banquet for his courtiers and officers and the leading men of Galilee. For when Herodias' daughter came in and danced, she pleased Herod and his guests;

and the king said to the girl, "Ask me for whatever you wish, and I will grant it." And he vowed to her, "Whatever you ask me, I will give you, even half of my kingdom." And she went out, and said to her mother, "What shall I ask?" And she said, "The head of John the baptizer." 25And she came in immediately with haste to the king, and asked, saying, "I want you to give me at once the head of John the Baptist on a platter." And the king was exceedingly sorry; but because of his oaths and his guests he did not want to break his word to her. And immediately the king sent a soldier of the guard and gave orders to bring his head. He went and beheaded him in the prison, and brought his head on a platter, and gave it to the girl; and the girl gave it to her mother. When his disciples heard of it, they came and took his body, and laid it in a tomb.

30The apostles returned to Jesus, and told him all that they had done and taught. And he said to them, "Come away by yourselves to a lonely place, and rest a while." For many were coming and going, and they had no leisure even to eat. And they went away in the boat to a lonely place by themselves. Now many saw them going, and knew them, and they ran there on foot from all the towns, and got there ahead of them. As he went ashore he saw a great throng, and he had compassion on them, because they were like sheep without a shepherd; and he began to teach them many things. 35And when it grew late, his disciples came to him and said, "This is a lonely place, and the hour is now late; send them away, to go into the country and villages round about and buy themselves something to eat." But he answered them, "You give them something to eat." And they said to him, "Shall we go and buy two hundred denarii worth of bread, and give it to them to eat?" And he said to them, "How many loaves have you? Go and see." And when they had found out, they said, "Five, and two fish." Then he commanded them all to sit down by companies upon the green grass. [40]So they sat down in groups, by hundreds and by fifties. And taking the five loaves and the two fish he looked up to heaven, and blessed, and broke the loaves, and gave them to the disciples to set before the people; and he divided the two fish among them all. And they all ate and were satisfied. And they took up twelve baskets full of broken pieces and of the fish. And those who ate the loaves were five thousand men.

[45]Immediately he made his disciples get into the boat and go before him to the other side, to Bethsaida, while he dismissed the crowd. And after he had taken leave of them, he went up on the mountain to pray. And when evening came, the boat was out on the sea, and he was alone on the land. And he saw that they were making headway painfully, for the wind was against them. And about the fourth watch of the night he came to them, walking on the sea. He meant to pass by them, but when they saw him walking on the sea they thought it was a ghost, and cried out; [50]for they all saw him, and were terrified. But immediately he spoke to them and said, "Take heart, it is I; have no fear." And he got into the boat with them and the wind ceased. And they were utterly astounded, for they did not understand about the loaves, but their hearts were hardened.

And when they had crossed over, they came to land at Gennesaret, and moored to the shore. And when they got out of the boat, immediately the people recognized him, [55]and ran about the whole neighborhood and began to bring sick people on their pallets to any place where they heard he was. And wherever he came, in villages, cities, or country, they laid the sick in the market places, and besought him that they might touch even the fringe of his garment; and as many as touched it were made well.

CHAPTER 7

Now when the Pharisees gathered together to him, with some of the scribes, who had come from Jerusalem, they saw that some of his disciples ate with hands defiled, that is, unwashed. (For the Pharisees, and all the Jews, do not eat unless they wash their hands, observing the tradition of the elders; and when they come from the market place, they do not eat unless they purify themselves; and there are many other traditions which they observe, the washing of cups and pots and vessels of bronze.) [5]And the Pharisees and the scribes asked him, "Why do your disciples not live according to the tradition of the elders, but eat with hands defiled?" And he said to them, "Well did Isaiah prophesy of you hypocrites, as it is written,

'This people honors me with their lips,
but their heart is far from me;
in vain do they worship me,
teaching as doctrines the precepts of men.'

You leave the commandment of God, and hold fast the tradition of men."

And he said to them, "You have a fine way of rejecting the commandment of God, in order to keep your tradition! [10]For Moses said, 'Honor your father and your mother'; and 'He who speaks evil of father or mother, let him surely die'; but you say, 'If a man tells his father or his mother, What you would have gained from me is Corban (that is, given to God)—

then you no longer permit him to do anything for his father
or mother, thus making void the word of God through your
tradition which you hand on. And many such things you do."

And he called the people to him again, and said to them,
"Hear me, all of you, and understand: [15]there is nothing outside a man which by going into him can defile him; but the
things which come out of a man are what defile him." And when
he had entered the house, and left the people, his disciples
asked him about the parable. And he said to them, "Then are
you also without understanding? Do you not see that whatever goes into a man from outside cannot defile him, since it
enters, not his heart but his stomach, and so passes on?" (Thus
he declared all foods clean.) [20]And he said, "What comes out
of a man is what defiles a man. For from within, out of the
heart of man, come evil thoughts, fornication, theft, murder,
adultery, coveting, wickedness, deceit, licentiousness, envy,
slander, pride, foolishness. All these evil things come from
within, and they defile a man."

And from there he arose and went away to the region of
Tyre and Sidon. And he entered a house, and would not have
any one know it; yet he could not be hid. [25]But immediately a
woman, whose little daughter was possessed by an unclean
spirit, heard of him, and came and fell down at his feet. Now the
woman was a Greek, a Syrophoenician by birth. And she
begged him to cast the demon out of her daughter. And he said
to her, "Let the children first be fed, for it is not right to take
the children's bread and throw it to the dogs." But she answered
him, "Yes, Lord; yet even the dogs under the table eat the children's crumbs." And he said to her, "For this saying you may go

your way; the demon has left your daughter." ³⁰And she went home, and found the child lying in bed, and the demon gone.

Then he returned from the region of Tyre, and went through Sidon to the Sea of Galilee, through the region of the Decapolis. And they brought to him a man who was deaf and had an impediment in his speech; and they besought him to lay his hand upon him. And taking him aside from the multitude privately, he put his fingers into his ears, and he spat and touched his tongue; and looking up to heaven, he sighed, and said to him, "Ephphatha," that is, "Be opened." ³⁵And his ears were opened, his tongue was released, and he spoke plainly. And he charged them to tell no one; but the more he charged them, the more zealously they proclaimed it. And they were astonished beyond measure, saying, "He has done all things well; he even makes the deaf hear and the dumb speak."

What's Happening Here?

Here begins a decisive, new direction in the ministry of Jesus. According to Mark he has been trying for some time to get away from the crowds, not because he's completely lost his popularity (even though his townspeople have just rejected him) but because the crowds continue to misinterpret his message about who he is. At this point in the gospel, Jesus succeeds in his desire to concentrate on instructing the disciples. This passage begins with the mission of the twelve, is interrupted by the report of the beheading of John the Baptist, and then proceeds to describe what has been called "the Loaves section," the recounting of the multiplication of the loaves, with its numerous sequels.

By comparison with Matthew's gospel, Mark's rendition of the mission of the twelve is brief, and it seems to be a preparation for Jesus' future self-revelation as the Messiah. Characteristically, Mark omits an instruction found in Matthew, that is, according to Matthew the disciples are not to go to the Gentiles. But since Mark is writing for Gentile readers, he skips that little detail. Also, in Luke's gospel the command to the disciples is to preach the coming of the reign of God. But here in Mark, the disciples are to preach repentance of sin. Mark reserves the proclamation of the reign of God to Jesus himself; therefore, the disciples are to be like John the Baptist, that is, to awaken the people to the fact that someone else (Jesus) is coming to proclaim the reign. The differences in these accounts may seem subtle, but the point is that these differences reflect various theological approaches used by the gospel writers. They are not all saying exactly the same thing, and we shouldn't expect that they would.

The next two verses (14-16) set the tone for much of what is to follow. The report here seems like gossip or, more exactly, a random poll of the reaction of the crowds about Jesus. These verses set the tone because they deal so directly with the question of the identity of Jesus. Those people who thought that Jesus was John risen from the dead obviously never saw the two together, but the identification of the two presumes that Jesus was considered a prophet like John, and also that John probably worked miracles like Jesus.

The rather detailed account of John's death is staged in three scenes. The first scene describes the accusation John made of Herod. The gospel maintains that Herod imprisoned John because the prophet denounced Herod's adultery. But it may also be true that Herod feared John because of John's disciples and his influence on the people. If this political motive was part of the intrigue, we have a much more complicated picture of the political climate of the times and the shaky security Herod felt as a puppet of the Romans. Scene two depicts Herodias tricking her husband into beheading John. What is significant here is that this whole episode is told in the light of the Old Testament book of Esther. The third scene foreshadows the burial of Jesus. In other words, Mark represents John's death in terms colored by the story of Esther and develops parallels between John and Jesus, particularly in the fact that John, like Jesus, was killed for his preaching.

The narrative resumes then with the return of the apostles from their mission. This is the only place in the gospel where Mark calls them apostles; he ordinarily refers to them as disciples, but since he just mentioned John's disciples, he probably uses the title "apostle" here to distinguish Jesus' followers from John's followers. Here "apostle" means "those sent out."

The passage entitled the Loaves section includes everything from chapter 6, verse 31, to chapter 8, verse 26. Two accounts of the multiplication of bread highlight this unit and each bread episode is followed by incidents recalling the multiplication.

Jesus leaves with the disciples, and when he attempts to be alone with them usually he is preparing them for a special revelation about himself. In Mark's view then, the feeding of the five thousand was performed primarily for the sake of the twelve. Jesus suggests that they rest for a while, probably because they are tired from their mission work. The rest period also adds an Old Testament dimension to the scene, particularly implying a shepherd theme. Jesus is like the good shepherd who gives his flock a rest. This shepherd theme continues throughout the passage, with overtones of the shepherd as the Messiah providing a Messianic banquet for his people. Jesus wants to bring God's word (food) to a hungry people. An obvious

Old Testament reference in this account is the story of the Israelites surviving on manna in the desert after they escaped from the Egyptians.

The actual multiplying of the loaves has been expanded by the early Church by adding details from the words used at the Eucharist. The twelve baskets of leftovers are a sign of God's fullness; there is enough for all, to feed all the people in the New Israel. Surprisingly, there is no remark about the crowd being amazed, as is the usual response to a Jesus miracle. The lack of this detail suggests that this multiplication episode is not meant precisely as a miracle, but as a sign to the twelve Apostles disclosing the secret of Jesus' identity as the Messiah.

The gospels of Matthew, Mark and Luke all include the miracle of Jesus walking on the water immediately after the story of the multiplication of the loaves. The connection between the two incidents becomes more emphatic when we place them side by side, one commenting on the other. Walking on the water is interpreted by the apostles as a sign of the Messiah, just like feeding the five thousand is a sign of the messianic banquet. The vocabulary and the description of the water scene indicates that this episode is especially designed to elicit a faith response, faith in Jesus as the Messiah. But Mark's conclusion states very clearly that the disciples still don't understand who Jesus is, even after the multiplication of the loaves and the walking on water. If they had really understood the message of the loaves, they would have known who it was coming to them on the water. Mark continually points out the disciples' inability to perceive the meaning of Jesus.

The popularity of Jesus reaches its high point after the feeding of the people in the desert. They recognize him everywhere and bring him the sick. He cures them, but Mark is not very enthusiastic about the way he presents these cures. He simply states it, in a tone that seems weary.

Jesus has just performed two dramatic signs of his identity as the Messiah. Now Mark introduces the Pharisees again, in order to demonstrate some of the differences between the teachings of the Jewish leaders and the teachings of Jesus' Messianic reign. The conflict here focuses on the unwritten laws of the Pharisees, laws which they observed with the same dedication as the written laws of Moses. Jesus insists on a distinction between these two kinds of regulations. He is in opposition to the legalism of the Pharisees.

In verse two the reference to the disciples eating meals is a link to the previous account of the feeding of the five thousand. Mark then adds a rather detailed explanation of these eating customs of the Jews, an explanation that would not be necessary if the readers were Jews themselves. The Pharisees are exposed as hypocrites in their worship, because they follow the regulations of man even when these rules contradict the commands of God. Jesus then gives an example of what he means. He refers to the practice of "korban" (Corban), the procedure of making a gift to God. Apparently, what some of the Pharisees were doing was offering their money as a gift to God. As a result they couldn't give it to anyone else, but they could use it themselves. They were using this practice of "korban" as an excuse for not helping their fathers and mothers, and there was no old age pension or social security in Jewish society. If the older parents were not cared for by their family there was no one to do it. They were poverty-stricken and neglected. The Pharisees were obviously violating the command of Moses and God to care for their parents, and doing so under the legal cover of "korban." Besides, they were probably bragging about their devotion in giving their money to God. Jesus' condemnation of them is strong and uncompromising.

The next section is quite clear in its insistence on man's evil coming from within himself, not from outside. In effect, Jesus internalizes the whole question of what constitutes sin. This passage is also significant in terms of the development of the gospel. Once again the disciples are alone with him, and Jesus uses the opportunity to inform them that in the new reign of God there will be a necessary reversal of values, a man will be responsible for the actions he himself initiates.

According to Mark, Jesus now switches his locality. He heads for the territory of the Gentiles, and the setting is provided for the primary message in this section: Jesus is Messiah not only for the Jews but for all men. Jesus is recognized again; the repeated mention of this recognition is building to a time when he will be recognized as the Messiah. At first Jesus refuses to help the Syro-Phoenician woman, perhaps in order to emphasize his unsuccessful attempt to convince Israel of his mission. They had a chance, more than any other nation, more than this Gentile woman. In any case, Jesus does help the woman; he is Messiah to the Gentiles as well.

The account which follows, the healing of the deaf-mute, has much the same lesson. It also reflects a Gentile setting and repeats the command to maintain the Messianic Secret. The reaction of the crowd is unusually strong; they "proclaim" what they have seen; proclamation being a Christian term for the good news about Jesus. The reference to Jesus "doing everything well" may be an allusion to the first book of the Bible, implying that Jesus has initiated a new creation.

Where Did This Message Come From?

Most of the words and actions of Jesus flowed from his desire to firmly establish the reign of God and to have that reign recognized and accepted by his followers. At least that's the way Matthew, Mark, and Luke present their gospels. John's gospel approaches the meaning of the life of Jesus from a different perspective. His view is more "poetic."

Mark makes use of the phrase, "the reign of God"

frequently. This phrase summarizes the core of Jesus' preaching, and as such it is a key concept in understanding the gospel. The meaning of this teaching is closely related to what we said earlier about the meaning of the title, "Messiah." The Messiah announces the new reign of God. Since the concept of the Messiah as popularly held by the crowds was considerably different, if not opposed to Jesus' view of the Messiah, it's not surprising that there would be significant variations between Jesus and the crowds about the nature of the reign of God as well.

It would seem helpful right at the beginning to clarify why the English translation, "the reign of God" is more acceptable than the more common phrase, "the kingdom of God." The term *kingdom* has a tendency to refer more specifically to the territory of the people ruled by a king. It's almost a passive term, which emphasizes "*being* ruled." And taken in that sense, it does not reflect the flavor of the original Greek word used by the evangelists. It's not completely inaccurate, but the words *reign* or *rule* or *kingship* are more accurate. In the original text, the Greek word meant more the state of being king, and therefore the emphasis was on the active force of the king. *Reign* captures that feeling of active rule more completely than does *kingdom*.

Another observation might be in order. Kings, reigns, and kingdoms are not a vital part of our culture. Even in those countries where there still are kings, the style of governing their subjects is greatly removed from the style

common in the middle East at the time of Jesus. As a
result we have very little experience of the nature of kingship as it's expressed in the gospels. We could think about
President, or Governor or Bishop or Pope, in an attempt
to relate to our own experience what the Bible means by
kingship. But here too, we have a difficult time getting
the idea across; there are too many distinctions that have
to be made with those titles. In a sense, we're forced back
to the gospel term with the hope that the primary thrust
of its message will strike us, even though the term *reign*
is somewhat foreign to our experience. The belief that
God is actively with us, as a community and through the
Holy Spirit is the kernel of the gospel message as expressed with the phrase "the reign of God."

There is no doubt that Jesus used the term "the
reign of God" in his preaching. Mark's gospel alone men-
tions that phrase fourteen times, most of the time in very
crucial passages. Jesus proclaims this reign from the
beginning of his public ministry, indicating that he saw
himself in a unique position; he was the one who was to
announce and usher in this new reign. He was a breakaway
from the age of the Old Testament; his mission was distinctive, he changed things radically. And yet he did not
wipe out the Old Testament tradition; he did not destroy
it. He claimed to fulfill it and to begin on a new plateau.
In some mysterious way the heavenly reality of God de-
scended into human history and became particularly
present in Jesus of Nazareth. Full participation in this
reign is reserved for heaven or to the end of the world
when all things will be completed according to the power

and designs of God. But the reign is a reality now as well. It is here, but it is not yet fully recognized or completely extended.

At the time of Jesus, the nation of Israel expected the coming reign of Yahweh. But the people expected that Israel would be in a unique position: They would rule the other nations politically, judging those countries, but not being judged themselves. God was on their side, and they were the fortunate, chosen ones. This arrangement, they believed, was the promise of Yahweh, and Yahweh simply can't fail because he's always faithful to his promises. They waited, they longed for this coming of the reign of God in order to get revenge on their enemies and also, in a more religious vein, to have their God Yahweh worshipped everywhere as the one true God.

In this highly explosive atmosphere, Jesus preached his type of reign. Most of the people couldn't buy it, but they did hear what he was claiming. When they crucified him, they charged him with the crime of claiming that he was the king of the Jews. They even made an inscription of this charge and nailed it to the cross. They knew what he was saying, but they didn't like his kind of king, a king who would have to suffer. If the king has to suffer, his followers will probably have to suffer also. *That* they could do without.

Jesus therefore eliminated many of the elements of Jewish expectations. One way of saying this is to point out a switch in emphasis. For the prophets of the Old

Testament and for Jesus, the reign of God would express the will of God for the nation of Israel. By the time of Jesus the people had switched it around; for them the reign of God meant that Yahweh would do the will of the people: The people, specifically the Jewish religious and political leaders, would determine what *they* wanted, and Yahweh became the means by which their purposes would be fulfilled. They wanted to control God. It's in this context that Jesus opposed and attacked the Pharisees. A good example of this conflict is found in chapter 7 of Mark's gospel.

Another important aspect of the reign of God as preached by Jesus is the call to repentance, to forgiveness. But the Jewish leaders didn't know what to be sorry for. Repent of what? They followed the law; they went to the temple and synagogue. They therefore felt they had a good relationship with God. In effect, Jesus was saying that the law was not a sure guide for behavior; it did not contain a complete statement about the will of God. More was demanded. The security felt by the Pharisees was a false security, and their holier-than-thou attitude was to be condemned. They too, as well as everyone else, must seek forgiveness, admitting that they at times can hurt their neighbors and thereby bring evil into the world. It's precisely this call for repentance that Jesus insists upon in his confrontation with the Pharisees regarding the practice of "korban." But they stubbornly refuse to admit their need for forgiveness, and for this reason the Pharisees cannot participate in the new reign of God.

According to Mark, Jesus then follows his call for repentance with another characteristic of the reign of God. The Master maintains that "what emerges from within a man, that and nothing else is what makes him unclean." In other words, personal decisions and the acceptance of personal responsibility for our actions is a quality needed for those who wish to belong to the reign. We cannot lose ourselves in the crowd, running with the herd, and expect to be saved. Membership in the group is not a substitute for personal decisions about our beliefs and our conduct. Religious routine, going through the motions, is not the hallmark of a true member of God's reign. Somewhere along the line we have to make our own personal decision regarding Jesus. Without this decision to accept or reject Jesus, we cannot really call ourselves Christians.

The reign of God is a term which includes and summarizes just about the whole of Jesus' preaching. As such, it has many aspects to it. In the stories about the multiplication of the loaves and the walking on the water, Jesus is trying through these events to announce that the reign of God is here in him, the Messiah. From the beginning of his gospel to its final verse, Mark is describing this reign, pointing to Jesus as the Messiah who brings it about, and inviting his readers to adopt those qualities of life which are in conformity with membership in that reign. We can read each episode of the gospel with this question in mind: What does this incident have to say about Jesus and the reign of God? Properly understood, they will all say something about it.

So What?

The United States is a melting pot. People from many nations, many cultures, with various styles of life and multiple value systems have settled on this large piece of land and tried to make it something of a home. Except for the Indians, we are all immigrants in this country, with an American history of a mere three hundred years. We came here with diverse backgrounds, hoping we could melt into some kind of effective unity while maintaining our personal and group values. It's debatable whether we, as a nation, have accomplished that goal.

This country is still a melting pot. People from different cultures still come to this land, bringing with them their desires and their way of life. But we are a melting pot from another point of view as well. There are many divergent ways of living within these boundaries, even for people who have lived here all their lives. An uptown Chicago resident will live a very different life than a Kansas farmer. A small town in Nebraska will house people with thoughts and feelings that could easily be foreign to inhabitants of New Orleans. The Californian way of life would be lost in Philadelphia. As a nation we are an amalgamation of many differences.

Add the whole world to the pot and it becomes even more evident that human beings are a complicated group of creatures, with so many diverse living patterns and behaviors that it seems impossible to offer something

THE NEW COLOSSUS.

NOT LIKE THE BRAZEN GIANT OF GREEK FAME,
WITH CONQUERING LIMBS ASTRIDE FROM LAND TO LAND;
HERE AT OUR SEA-WASHED, SUNSET GATES SHALL STAND
A MIGHTY WOMAN WITH A TORCH, WHOSE FLAME
IS THE IMPRISONED LIGHTNING, AND HER NAME
MOTHER OF EXILES. FROM HER BEACON-HAND
GLOWS WORLD-WIDE WELCOME; HER MILD EYES COMMAND
THE AIR-BRIDGED HARBOR THAT TWIN CITIES FRAME
"KEEP ANCIENT LANDS, YOUR STORIED POMP!"
    CRIES SHE
WITH SILENT LIPS. "GIVE ME YOUR TIRED, YOUR
    POOR,
YOUR HUDDLED MASSES YEARNING TO BREATHE FREE,
THE WRETCHED REFUSE OF YOUR TEEMING SHORE.
SEND THESE, THE HOMELESS, TEMPEST-TOST TO ME,
I LIFT MY LAMP BESIDE THE GOLDEN DOOR!"

THIS TABLET, WITH HER SONNET TO THE BARTHOLDI STATUE
OF LIBERTY ENGRAVED UPON IT, IS PLACED UPON THESE WALLS
IN LOVING MEMORY OF
EMMA LAZARUS
BORN IN NEW YORK CITY, JULY 22ᵈ, 1849
DIED NOVEMBER 19ᵗʰ, 1887.

which everyone could appreciate and find helpful. A message for all men seems doomed to failure.

And yet it's precisely that kind of universal message Jesus offered. The proclamation of "the reign of God" is meant for all people, in whatever situation they find themselves. All too often in the course of history that message has become so involved in a particular culture that the basic theme of the gospel is hidden, disguised by cultural habits, by ways of speaking, by unessential practices which interfere with the simple joyful announcement that God is truly with us.

There are many people in this world whose primary concern and legitimate worry is where a meager allotment of food is coming from for that day. For these millions, the name of the game is simple survival. For others, food on the table is taken for granted; their major worries center on family life, job satisfaction, and the relationships they form with society as a whole and with friends in particular. And yet for both these groups and for everyone in between these groups, the message of Jesus is intended, the person of Jesus is offered.

The incident recounting the multiplication of the loaves invites these reflections on the diverse types of people in this world of ours. The story insists that there is food for all in the reign of God. The reference is not just to physical food, though feeding the hungry is a basic command for those who believe in Jesus. The reference is to hope arising from faith and expressing itself in charity. It's a hope that stubbornly refuses to give up on God in the midst of poverty, a hope that provides encouragement to those Christians seeking some kind of basic unity amid all the diversity.

What can the individual do to actively cooperate in extending the reign of God? The individual can first of all look around him and listen to the needs of the people near him. He can share what he hears with others, perhaps they too recognize the same needs. He can then look to himself and determine his own talents. He can offer his talents to those in need, in whatever way he can. Usually this process of determining the needs of people and discovering our own talents (which we all have) is much more effective when done with a small group of people. What the group decides to do to help extend the reign of God will vary; there are many possibilities. Some decide to visit the elderly on a regular basis; some become committed to improving housing conditions in their neighborhood; others find ways to ease racial tension; some join the fight against pollution; still others concentrate on feeding the hungry. There are innumerable possibilities, and everyone can do something. The important thing is to do something constructive, and do it believing that God is present to all men offering his comfort and his challenge.

CHAPTER SIX

Finally, Recognition!

Mark 8:1-30

CHAPTER 8

In those days, when again a great crowd had gathered, and they had nothing to eat, he called his disciples to him, and said to them, "I have compassion on the crowd, because they have been with me now three days, and have nothing to eat; and if I send them away hungry to their homes, they will faint on the way; and some of them have come a long way." And his disciples answered him, "How can one feed these men with bread here in the desert?" [5]And he asked them, "How many loaves have you?" They said, "Seven." And he commanded the crowd to sit down on the ground; and he took the seven loaves, and having given thanks he broke them and gave them to his disciples to set before the people; and they set them before the crowd. And they had a few small fish; and having blessed them, he commanded that these also should be set before them. And they ate, and were satisfied; and they took up the broken pieces left over, seven baskets full. And there were about four thousand people. [10]And he sent them away; and immediately he got into the boat with his disciples, and went to the district of Dalmanutha.

The Pharisees came and began to argue with him, seeking from him a sign from heaven, to test him. And he sighed deeply in his spirit, and said, "Why does this generation seek a sign? Truly, I say to you, no sign shall be given to this generation." And he left them, and getting into the boat again he departed to the other side.

Now they had forgotten to bring bread; and they had only one loaf with them in the boat. [15]And he cautioned them, saying, "Take heed, beware of the leaven of the Pharisees and the leaven of Herod." And they discussed it with one another, saying, "We have no bread." And being aware of it, Jesus said to them, "Why do you discuss the fact that you have no bread? Do you not yet perceive or understand? Are your hearts hardened? Having eyes do you not see, and having ears do you not hear? And do you not remember? When I broke the five loaves for the five thousand, how many baskets full of broken pieces did you take up?" They said to him, "Twelve." 20"And the seven for the four thousand, how many baskets full of broken pieces did you take up?" And they said to him, "Seven." And he said to them, "Do you not yet understand?"

And they came to Bethsaida. And some people brought to him a blind man, and begged him to touch him. And he took the blind man by the hand, and led him out of the village; and when he had spit on his eyes and laid his hands upon him, he asked him, "Do you see anything?" And he looked up and said, "I see men; but they look like trees, walking. 25Then again he laid his hands upon his eyes; and he looked intently and was restored, and saw everything clearly. And he sent him away to his home, saying, "Do not even enter the village."

And Jesus went on with his disciples, to the villages of Caesarea Philippi; and on the way he asked his disciples, "Who do men say that I am?" And they told him, "John the Baptist; and others say, Elijah; and others one of the prophets." And he asked them, "But who do you say that I am?" Peter answered him, "You are the Christ." 30And he charged them to tell no one about him.

What's Happening Here?

The Secret is out. In this section of Mark's gospel, someone finally recognizes Jesus as the Messiah or the Christ (Messiah is a Hebrew word; Christ is a Greek word with the same meaning). The someone is Peter. The place is Caesarea Philippi. It's not a public pronouncement exactly; the only audience is the other eleven disciples. But it is the first real profession of faith in Jesus as the Messiah. More than likely, the episode at Caesarea Philippi was not just a sudden burst of insight on the part of Peter; he and the other disciples probably discussed the possibility of Jesus as Messiah before he makes this straightforward profession when Jesus puts the question to him. It's not an admission in the divinity of Jesus, and the disciples still don't understand the kind of Messiah Jesus is, but it's a beginning. According to Mark, it's this kind of beginning Jesus was looking for.

Before this central event takes place, Mark recounts a few preparatory incidents. In one sense the first eight chapters of the gospel is preparing for Peter's statement; each previous episode is building towards this conclusion. But immediately preceding the confession at Caesarea Philippi, Mark records three significant incidents which in a particular and dramatic way lead into Peter's faith-statement. There is first of all the second accounting of the multiplication of the loaves. Secondly, there's a section describing the blindness of the disciples, and this is followed immediately with the story about the blind man of Bethsaida. It's with this climactic order that Mark dramatizes the importance of Peter's recognition of Jesus as the Messiah.

In Mark there are two accounts of the multiplication of the loaves. Most likely this second story is another version of the same miracle, retold here in order to emphasize the significance of the multiplication (as a preview of the Eucharist) and to provide a Gentile setting for this feeding miracle. In other words, the first account of the loaves and fishes was for the Jews; this second rendition is for the Gentiles. Mark, as we have seen, is particularly concerned about including the Gentiles within his gospel. In that framework it is perfectly understandable that he would retell the multiplication incident again. It fits his theological purposes to emphasize the account by repeating it.

The feeding of the four thousand takes place in pagan territory, and that note about the location is one of the most important aspects of these thirteen verses. Compared with the first account of the multiplication of the loaves, the approach here de-emphasizes the role of the disciples and therefore highlights the role of Jesus. The previous account also introduced the Old Testament theme of Jesus as shepherd to his flock. That thematic reference is absent from this second version of the story, probably because the setting here is Gentile territory. There is mention of a multiplication of a few small fish as well, but it's almost an afterthought; the emphasis is on the bread, since bread was more widely used for the Eucharist in the early Church. The basic message here is the same as in the first version of the multiplication of the bread: Jesus is the bread of life, providing food for all. The reign of God has come, and Jesus alone can satisfy man's need for food.

The Pharisees are not impressed with the signs Jesus has been giving them about his Messiahship. They ask for still another sign, but Jesus refuses since their motivation is to "test him," that is, to trap him. The sign they want corresponds to the kind of Messiah they expect, and as such they are in opposition to Jesus. He works no such sign, implying that they don't have true faith in Jesus, that their style of religion is a dead end, and that God will not work according to their demands.

The next section contains a stern rebuke to the disciples for their lack of understanding the meaning of the multiplication of the loaves. The reference to the yeast of the Pharisees and Herod does not really fit here, but it seems to be included because it deals with bread. In any case, this "evil" yeast has the power to infect even the disciples and it's a reminder to the reader that the forces of evil are still at work.

The blindness of the disciples is evident in this passage. They forget to bring bread for the trip, an obvious allusion to the previous two episodes of the multiplication of the bread. They continue to think of the bread in a strictly physical sense, thereby missing the meaning of the message, that Jesus is the bread of life. Jesus asks them to remember those two miracles with the hope that by remembering, they will see who he is, that is, recognize him as the Messiah.

The story of the curing of the blind man is similar to the story of the healing of the deaf-mute which followed the first account of the multiplication miracle. The cure here, as recorded by Mark, takes place gradually, the only place in the gospel where this happens. There are probably two reasons why this healing is recounted here. First of all, in the Old Testament it was stated that a sign of the Messiah would be that he would bring hearing to the deaf and sight to the blind. Following the first multiplication of the bread, Mark tells the story of Jesus bringing hearing to the deaf. Following the second account of the multiplication, Mark includes the cure of the blind man; Jesus brings sight to the blind. In effect then, these two healings are a sign of his Messiahship, fulfilling the prediction of the Old Testament.

The second reason why this cure of the blind man is placed in this part of the gospel is due to its gradual nature. There is a similarity between the gradual restoration of sight to the blind man and the gradual recognition of Jesus as Messiah by the disciples. The disciples are blinded to the fact of Jesus' identity. Jesus has to repeat himself before they begin to get the message. Jesus likewise repeats himself as he gradually opens the eyes of the blind man.

The next passage (chapter 8, verses 27-30) is the turning point in the gospel of Mark. It's the hinge on which everything revolves. "Who do you say that I am?" It's the big question—the only question, really. The disciples proudly assert their fumbling faith: "You are the Messiah." Once the disciples, with Peter as their spokesman, recognize Jesus as the Messiah, the gospel proceeds with a renewed fervor, with a thrust and a vision that reverses man's usual sense of values. That new direction is introduced almost immediately: The Messiah will have to suffer. The disciples apparently did not understand this element of suffering, even as they admitted the Messiahship of Jesus. Jesus therefore still requires them to keep silent about who he is; he has to teach them further, correcting any false impressions they may have about his Messiahship. In a real sense, though, Jesus has been successful in his previous teaching. Other men don't even think of him as Messiah. To them he is John the Baptist or Elijah or someone else, but not the Messiah. Jesus' earlier decision to concentrate on teaching the disciples about his true identity is beginning to pay off in their recognition of him as Messiah, even though their idea of Messiahship must still be corrected.

Where Did This Message Come From?

In general, men have always been believers. Primitive man believed in a spirit-world, a world existing beyond and behind a visible creation. The popularity and extension of the many world religions, both present and past, attest to the religious convictions of most men. People who have not aligned themselves to an organized religion oftentimes give evidence that they too are faith-people; they believe in something beyond themselves. The experience of faith has been with man since the beginning, is still present, and promises to remain a part of man's life.

There are of course differences about the nature of faith, its importance in an individual's life, ways of expressing it, and who or what to believe in. For example, there are similarities between Buddhists and Christians, and fortunately these similarities are being examined and shared more extensively now than in the past. But there are differences between Buddhists and Christians as well, just like there are differences between all religions. In terms of the faith question, the same thing could be said. There are major areas of agreement between religions regarding the nature of faith, and yet there remains simultaneously areas of differences. This co-existence of similarities and dissimilarities regarding the experience of faith should not be surprising, since faith is such an important aspect of life.

The gospel of Mark was written by a man of faith and intended to inspire faith in its readers. Faith is a dimension of the book that cannot really be eliminated. The gospel could be studied strictly as literature but that approach would be like studying an automobile mechanics manual as poetry. It doesn't really work; the purpose of the gospel is to talk about faith and to hopefully elicit faith in those who hear it.

The faith of the gospel is a specific kind of faith. It maintains, first of all, that there is a God. An atheist might read the gospel and be inspired by the concern Jesus showed to other people, by the courage and convictions he lived and died for, and by the loyalty of his followers. But an atheist (a person who doesn't believe in the existence of God) would necessarily miss a crucial dimension of the gospel, namely, that there is a God who is concerned about man. The faith of the gospel goes further; it boldly states that Jesus of Nazareth is this God made man who offers to all men the hope that life has meaning, a meaning focused on Jesus. Mark's little book also insists that the Holy Spirit, sent by Jesus to be permanently present in this world, will continue to enliven mankind with the consistent message and power that God is with us, loving, forgiving, and saving us. It's this kind of belief that Mark gives testimony to, and it's out of this faith-framework that he writes his book.

The experience of faith has many qualities to it. It is primarily an experience; it is not just intellectually stating the propositions about God and Church which have been handed down to us. A person could state those ideas and not really experience them. A faith experience implies an acceptance by the whole person; mind, emotions, feelings, desires must all in some way participate in a genuine faith-experience. Such a faith-experience can be a very dramatic one-time episode, as St. Paul apparently experienced on the road to Damascus, when he was thrown from his horse and changed the direction of his life. Or a faith-experience can be a slowly developing sense of conviction, something that may take years and many contributing events. But genuine gospel faith is something that is lasting; it's not just a "spiritual high." It implies a way of life, a code of conduct, and a desire to renew and deepen the faith convictions. In terms of the gospel, faith means a consistently growing conviction that the Resurrection of Jesus provides meaning for a person's life. Jesus rose from the dead and that belief infiltrates the life of a gospel believer.

Jesus asks for faith from his followers. This is evident from almost every passage in the gospel. He works cures, but only on the condition that the recipient expresses some kind of faith in Jesus. He spends hours, days, months with his disciples, giving them many opportunities to believe in him. He finally asks them point blank: Who am I? Peter responds with the faith statement that Jesus is the Messiah. Eliciting faith is one of Jesus' major concerns.

And yet Jesus never forces faith. He invites it, he encourages it, he points to the benefits a believer can lay claim to, but he doesn't take away the freedom of the potential believer. With every cure he asks for faith, but when his townspeople give no evidence of any faith in him, he "could work no miracles there." He is extremely patient with his disciples, even though they consistently miss his message. He does not force them. At one point, he confronts them very seriously with the ultimate statement of freedom: "Do you want to leave me also?" In other words, "You are free to go. Don't stay with me just because you feel you 'have' to." Judas is one of his chosen twelve, and Jesus does not interfere with that follower's decision to betray the Master. Jesus respects the freedom of all men, and that respect is one of the amazing features of his personality.

For any faith to be genuine a similar atmosphere of freedom must be present. An individual must know the alternatives and freely choose to believe. After the crucifixion, Peter returns to his fishing. He was free to do so; in effect his return to fishing was a continued denial of his faith in Jesus. He could have spent the rest of his life fishing, but when he met the resurrected Lord, he made his free decision to believe again, this time a permanent decision. Apparently most of the other disciples experienced a similar freedom; they could either follow Jesus or reject him; it was up to them. Jesus simply offered himself, his message to them. Eventually he made that message clear to them, but once again, he never forced them. Many other people heard Jesus, saw him, marveled at his message and stood in amazement at his power, but quite obviously never became his disciples. They freely chose to either forget Jesus or to reject him. Whatever the case, Jesus did not chase after them and insist, for their own good, that they believe in him. He let them go. For Jesus, a faith commitment must be made freely, or else it runs the risk of not being genuine.

Another dimension of faith as described in the gospel of Mark is its communitarian feature. The individual must make his own personal faith decision, but oftentimes the individual is living in and influenced by a community. The disciples themselves were something of a community: They experienced Jesus together; they all walked with him and witnessed much of his life as a group. Undoubtedly they talked about this Jesus among themselves; they compared insights and ideas, they were puzzled together, they were afraid together, and they misunderstood together. Jesus rebuked them as a group and he taught them as a group. They were a community to the point of accepting Peter as their spokesman—or at least they did not object to Peter speaking for them. When Peter expressed his belief that Jesus was the Messiah, he did so in the name of the other eleven. He made his personal decision regarding Jesus, as presumably the other men did, but he made that faith commitment in the context of the community of the disciples.

An authentic gospel faith reflects this community dimension. No one is completely isolated from other men; we are social beings. Others influence us, some more than others. Family, friends, people we contact are all possible influences on our lives. We are more or less products of the effects these people have on us. In some form or another, Christianity has always maintained this communitarian aspect of life. The followers of Jesus have done so because they experience Jesus that way themselves and because they recognize that they would need each other for mutual support and encouragement as they attempt to deepen their faith and live their Christian lives ever more faithfully. That's why the early Christians formed communities wherever they could: They needed each other and they believed that the Holy Spirit was present to them not just as individuals but as members of the community.

The gospel then, to be fully appreciated, must be read by a believer. The question Jesus confronted the disciples with—"Who do you say that I am?"—is a question directed to the reader as well as to the disciples. It's an inquiry that challenges, that puts us on the spot. But it's a question that respects our freedom while at the same time admitting our need for a community, for the influence and support of other people. It's a puzzling, demanding, crucial faith question.

So What?

For many people, decision-making is one of the most difficult activities in life. Should I continue with my schooling? Should I look for a job? What kind of job? Should I get married? When? And to whom? How much control do I want of my own future? What kind of life style do I want to live? The possibilities go on and on: major decisions and minor ones. They face us whether we want them or not. How we make those decisions and what we do with them after we've made them contribute greatly to our happiness or disappointment with life.

It seems that some people simply "find" themselves living the results of things that happen to them, without making much of a conscious effort at deciding what they want and what is best. A young couple may "drift" into marriage, not considering the responsibilities involved. A high school graduate may go to college because other people go to college. A man may take a job because he doesn't want to bother looking for a different job, one that would bring him more satisfaction. The root problem in these and other similar situations is an inability to make effective decisions.

To help himself make a good decision, an individual could gather as much information as he can about the situation, talking with other people who have experience in the area, and reading pertinent material related to the decision. He can then sort out all the information he has gathered and establish those facets of the evidence which he considers most important and those which he considers least important. He determines his priorities. The next step in this decision-making process would be to investigate as clearly as possible the consequences of the decision: "If I decide this way, then what follows? If I decide the other way, what would be the results? I think ahead." Finally, after gathering and studying and discussing as many of the implications as he can, he makes the decision. Once made, he sticks to it. There remains, of course, the possibility that later on, new information may indicate that a different decision may be made. In that case, the whole process could begin again. But this procedure, or a similar one could help people in the difficulties they experience as they make decisions.

Religion is one area of life where it appears that many people don't seem to make much of a decision. They either "drift" into it or "drift" away from it. In the first case, they remain a visible part of an organized religion because it's expected of them or because they've always done it. Drifting away from religion takes place when a person simply doesn't feel like becoming involved in it or gives up on it without seriously considering what it's really all about. In both cases, in either drifting into it or drifting away from it, the person doesn't seem to make much of a decision about it. It "just happens."

Read correctly, the gospel of Mark doesn't allow this slip-shod decision-making to happen. It confronts us with the faith question and insists that we answer it, that we make a decision about it. "Who do you say that I am?" Jesus asks. Taken seriously, that one line forces us to make up our minds about Jesus and about Christianity.

For many American Christians the decision about faith is complicated by the fact that many of us are "born into a religion." As children we are influenced by the religious style of our parents. This influence is legitimate — and in any case it's unavoidable. Parents share their convictions with their children, consciously or unconsciously. The faith of the parents, whether it is genuine, indifferent, or hypocritical, will necessarily affect the children. The real difficulty emerges when the children approach or reach adulthood. Sometime in that growth process from childhood to adulthood the individual will have to make a decision about his faith, a personal decision. Without that step, without that personal involvement, the individual will never reach the level of adult faith, a faith that unifies and provides meaning for his life. This confrontation with faith may take some time, maybe years as it did with the disciples, but it has to be there somewhere. Otherwise, the result is an adult who exhibits "childish faith" or a person who rejects faith for all the "wrong" reasons. And like any other effective decision, this one must be made in the atmosphere of freedom. If there isn't a large dose of freedom mixed in with this decision or if the individual doesn't know how to responsibly handle that freedom, the crucial question regarding religion is left unanswered. The response to Jesus' basic inquiry—"Who do you say that I am?"—then becomes an insignificant shrug of the shoulders.

CHAPTER SEVEN

Yes, But . . .

8:31

And he began to teach them that the Son of man must suffer many things, and be rejected by the elders and the chief priests and the scribes, and be killed, and after three days rise again. And he said this plainly. And Peter took him, and began to rebuke him. But turning and seeing his disciples, he rebuked Peter, and said, "Get behind me, Satan! For you are not on the side of God, but of men."

And he called to him the multitude with his disciples, and said to them, "If any man would come after me, let him deny himself and take up his cross and follow me. [35]For whoever would save his life will lose it; and whoever loses his life for my sake and the gospel's will save it. For what does it profit a man, to gain the whole world and forfeit his life? For what can a man give in return for his life? For whoever is ashamed of me and of my words in this adulterous and sinful generation, of him will the Son of man also be ashamed, when he comes in the glory of his Father with the holy angels."

CHAPTER 9

And he said to them, "Truly, I say to you, there are some standing here who will not taste death before they see the kingdom of God has come with power."

And after six days Jesus took with him Peter and James and John, and led them up a high mountain apart by themselves; and he was transfigured before them, and his garments became glistening, intensely white, as no fuller on earth could bleach them. And there appeared to them Elijah with Moses; and they were talking to Jesus. [5]And Peter said to Jesus,

"Master, it is well that we are here; let us make three booths, one for you and one for Moses and one for Elijah." For he did not know what to say, for they were exceedingly afraid. And a cloud overshadowed them, and a voice came out of the cloud, "This is my beloved Son; listen to him." And suddenly looking around they no longer saw any one with them but Jesus only.

And as they were coming down the mountain, he charged them to tell no one what they had seen, until the Son of man should have risen from the dead. [10]So they kept the matter to themselves, questioning what the rising from the dead meant. And they asked him, "Why do the scribes say that first Elijah must come?" And he said to them, "Elijah does come first to restore all things; and how is it written of the Son of man, that he should suffer many things and be treated with contempt? But I tell you that Elijah has come, and they did to him whatever they pleased, as it is written of him."

And when they came to the disciples, they saw a great crowd about them, and scribes arguing with them. [15]And immediately all the crowd, when they saw him, were greatly amazed, and ran up to him and greeted him. And he asked them, "What are you discussing with them?" And one of the crowd answered him, "Teacher, I brought my son to you, for he has a dumb spirit; and wherever it seizes him, it dashes him down; and he foams and grinds his teeth and becomes rigid; and I asked your disciples to cast it out, and they were not able." And he answered them, "O faithless generation, how long am I to be with you? How long am I to bear with you? Bring him to me." [20]And they brought the boy to him; and when the spirit saw him, immediately it convulsed the boy, and he fell on the ground and rolled about, foaming at the mouth. And Jesus asked his father, "How long has he had this?" And he said, "From childhood. And it has often cast him into the fire and into the water, to destroy him; but if you can do anything, have pity on us and help us." And Jesus said to him, "If you can! All things are possible to him who believes." Immediately the father of the child cried out and said, "I believe; help my unbelief!" 25And when Jesus saw that a crowd came running together, he rebuked the unclean spirit, saying to it, "You dumb and deaf spirit, I command you, come out of him, and never enter him again." And after crying out and convulsing him terribly, it came out, and the boy was like a corpse; so that most of them said, "He is dead." But Jesus took him by the hand and lifted him up, and he arose. And when he had entered the house, his disciples asked him privately, "Why could we not cast it out?" And he said to them, "This kind cannot be driven out by anything but prayer."

30They went on from there and passed through Galilee. And he would not have any one know it; for he was teaching his disciples, saying to them, "The Son of man will be delivered into the hands of men, and they will kill him; and when he is killed, after three days he will rise." But they did not understand the saying, and they were afraid to ask him.

And they came to Capernaum; and when he was in the house he asked them, "What were you discussing on the way?" But they were silent; for on the way they had discussed with one another who was the greatest. 35And he sat down and called the twelve; and he said to them, "If any one would be first, he must be last of all and servant of all." And he took a child, and put him in the midst of them; and taking him in his arms, he said to them, "Whoever receives one such child in my name receives me; and whoever receives me, receives not me but him who sent me."

John said to him, "Teacher, we saw a man casting out demons in your name, and we forbade him, because he was not following us." But Jesus said, "Do not forbid him; for no one who does a mighty work in my name will be able soon after to speak evil of me. ⁴⁰For he that is not against us is for us. For truly, I say to you, whoever gives you a cup of water to drink because you bear the name of Christ, will by no means lose his reward.

"Whoever causes one of these little ones who believe in me to sin, it would be better for him if a great millstone were hung round his neck and he were thrown into the sea. And if your hand causes you to sin, cut it off; it is better for you to enter life maimed than with two hands to go to hell, to the un-quenchable fire. ⁴⁵And if your foot causes you to sin, cut it off; it is better for you to enter life lame than with two feet to be thrown into hell. And if your eye causes you to sin, pluck it out; it is better for you to enter the kingdom of God with one eye than with two eyes to be thrown into hell, where their worm does not die, and the fire is not quenched. For every one will be salted with fire. ⁵⁰Salt is good; but if the salt has lost its saltness, how will you season it? Have salt in yourselves, and be at peace with one another."

CHAPTER 10

And he left there and went to the region of Judea and beyond the Jordan, and crowds gathered to him again; and again, as his custom was, he taught them.

And Pharisees came up and in order to test him asked, "Is it lawful for a man to divorce his wife?" He answered them, "What did Moses command you?" They said, "Moses allowed a man to write a certificate of divorce, and to put her away." 5But Jesus said to them, "For your hardness of heart he wrote you this commandment. But from the beginning of creation, 'God made them male and female.' 'For this reason a man shall leave his father and mother and be joined to his wife, and the two shall become one.' So they are no longer two but one. What therefore God has joined together, let not man put asunder."

10And in the house the disciples asked him again about this matter. And he said to them, "Whoever divorces his wife and marries another, commits adultery against her; and if she divorces her husband and marries another, she commits adultery."

And they were bringing children to him, that he might touch them; and the disciples rebuked them. But when Jesus saw it he was indignant, and said to them, "Let the children come to me, do not hinder them; for to such belongs the kingdom of God. 15Truly, I say to you, whoever does not receive the kingdom of God like a child shall not enter it." And he took them in his arms and blessed them, laying his hands upon them.

And as he was setting out on his journey, a man ran up and knelt before him, and asked him, "Good Teacher, what must I do to inherit eternal life?" And Jesus said to him, "Why do you call me good? No one is good but God alone. You know the commandments: 'Do not kill, Do not commit adultery, Do not steal, Do not bear false witness, Do not defraud, Honor your father and mother.'" [20]And he said to him, "Teacher, all these I have observed from my youth." And Jesus looking upon him loved him, and said to him, "You lack one thing; go, sell what you have, and give to the poor, and you will have treasure in heaven; and come, follow me." At that saying his countenance fell, and he went away sorrowful; for he had great possessions.

And Jesus looked around and said to his disciples, "How hard it will be for those who have riches to enter the kingdom of God!" And the disciples were amazed at his words. But Jesus said to them again, "Children, how hard it is to enter the kingdom of God! [25]It is easier for a camel to go through the eye of a needle than for a rich man to enter the kingdom of God." And they were exceedingly astonished, and said to him, "Then who can be saved?" Jesus looked at them and said, "With men it is impossible, but not with God; for all things are possible with God." Peter began to say to him, "Lo, we have left everything and followed you." Jesus said, "Truly, I say to you, there is no one who has left house or brothers or sisters or mother or father or children or lands, for my sake and for the gospel, [30]who will not receive a hundredfold now in this time, houses and brothers and sisters and mothers and children and lands, with persecutions, and in the age to come eternal life. But many that are first will be last, and the last first."

And they were on the road, going up to Jerusalem, and Jesus was walking ahead of them; and they were amazed, and those who followed were afraid. And taking the twelve again, he began to tell them what was to happen to him, saying, "Behold, we are going up to Jerusalem; and the Son of man will be delivered to the chief priests and the scribes, and they will condemn him to death, and deliver him to the Gentiles; and they will mock him, and spit upon him, and scourge him, and kill him; and after three days he will arise."

[35]And James and John, the sons of Zebedee, came forward to him, and said to him, "Teacher, we want you to do for us whatever we ask of you." And he said to them, "What do you want me to do for you?" And they said to him, "Grant us to sit, one at your right hand and one at your left, in your glory." But Jesus said to them, "You do not know what you are asking. Are you able to drink the cup that I drink, or to be baptized with the baptism with which I am baptized?" And they said to him, "We are able." And Jesus said to them, "The cup that I drink you will drink; and with the baptism with which I am baptized, you will be baptized; [40]but to sit at my right hand or at my left is not mine to grant, but it is for those for whom it has been prepared." And when the ten heard it, they began to be indignant at James and John. And Jesus called them to him and said to them, "You know that those who are supposed to rule over the Gentiles lord it over them, and their great men exercise authority over them. But it shall not be so among you; but whoever would be great among you must be your servant, and whoever would be first among you must be slave of all. [45]For the Son of man also came not to be served but to serve, and to give his life as a ransom for many."

And they came to Jericho; and as he was leaving Jericho

with his disciples and a great multitude, Bartimaeus, a blind beggar, the son of Timaeus, was sitting by the roadside. And when he heard that it was Jesus of Nazareth, he began to cry out and say, "Jesus, Son of David, have mercy on me!" And many rebuked him, telling him to be silent; but he cried out all the more, "Son of David, have mercy on me!" And Jesus stopped and said, "Call him." And they called the blind man, saying to him, "Take heart; rise, he is calling you." [50]And throwing off his mantle he sprang up and came to Jesus. And Jesus said to him, "What do you want me to do for you?" And the blind man said to him, "Master, let me receive my sight." And Jesus said to him, "Go your way; your faith has made you well." And immediately he received his sight and followed him on the way.

What's Happening Here?

This section of the gospel is a long one, and it should be kept together because Mark wrote it as a unit. It's developed around the three predictions of the passion of Jesus. After each prediction, Mark records the disciples' reaction which continues to be misunderstanding and disbelief. Jesus then proceeds to instruct the disciples, sometimes by word and sometimes by deed.

Immediately after Peter confesses to the Messiahship of Jesus, Mark includes the first prediction of the passion, death, and resurrection of Jesus. The purpose of this passage is obvious: Jesus must correct any false idea the disciples may have about the Messiah. He must attempt to give them some inkling of a suffering Messiah. These predictions have undoubtedly been reworked by the early Church and given their final form by Mark himself. It was only after the actual events of the passion and resurrection that the followers of Jesus could look back and say in effect, "Oh yes, he did give us a hint that he was going to die and rise, but we really didn't believe it." As a result, the structure of these predictions has been formed by the faith and with the hindsight of the early Church. The evidence indicates however that Jesus himself did say something regarding his coming fate.

From this point on in the gospel, Jesus will refer to himself as "the Son of Man." This title comes from the Old Testament and it refers primarily to the Jewish belief in the coming glory of a man who will act as judge of all nations. It indicates a glorious age for Israel. But the way Jesus uses this title adds another dimension to it. Jesus accepts the glory but he fuses the "Son of Man" with the notion of a "suffering Servant," another Old Testament title which many Jews conveniently forgot. In other words, Jesus claims glory, but insists on the suffering as well.

Mark then makes it very plain that the disciples needed instruction on the meaning of Messiah. The same Peter who just a few verses earlier proudly professed his belief in the Messiahship of Jesus is here strongly rebuked because he tried to talk Jesus out of the necessity of suffering. Peter in effect plays Satan's role, tempting Jesus to compromise his mission, to submit to the power of evil. Jesus replies that he'll have none of it, that the only effective way to overcome the evil of suffering and death is to accept it and then to defeat it on its own terms.

This episode leads naturally into a series of sayings and incidents related to commitment and discipleship. The task of discipleship is not a half-hearted job; it is a demanding life of dedication. But those who accept it whole-heartedly will receive their reward, a purposeful meaning in this life and a completeness in the next life.

The transfiguration of Jesus is another one of those episodes which is hard to reconstruct as it actually happened. Apparently something happened which gave the "favored" disciples, Peter, James, and John, an insight into the glory of this Messiah-Jesus. It is connected with the profession of Peter at Caesarea Philippi; it is described as taking place "six days later," and therefore it is a way of clarifying the kind of Messiah Jesus was. Jesus has accepted the title of Messiah; he then insists that he must also suffer. But here in the transfiguration he reinforces the notion that the Messiah is equally a man of glory. As such, this is a central event in describing the nature of Jesus' Messiahship.

This story is told in the context of many Old Testament themes. Moses and Elijah are there—Moses as the great Lawgiver and Elijah as a representative of all the Old Testament prophets. Jesus, then, is the fulfillment of the Law and the Prophets. Jesus was at least equal to those two highly respected people of Jewish history. Peter feels that the end of the world has come, the time of completeness, the time of fulfilled glory, and he wants to freeze that moment. In a sense, he over-reacts. The dazzling white, the cloud, the voice from the cloud, are all Old Testament images which refer to the special protective presence of God. Moses and Elijah leave, giving way to Jesus. Coming down the mountain, Jesus once again instructs them to keep the "Messianic Secret," though this time he adds the remark that there will be a future time when they can and should share this experience with others.

The question of the coming of Elijah was a current issue at the time of Jesus. The disciples are confused: they think that Jesus might just be Elijah. But Jesus corrects them by saying that Elijah has already come, the most obvious reference being to John the Baptist. John was a prophet in the same tradition as Elijah. The common expectation shared by the disciples was that the self-same man named Elijah would come. Jesus denies that, but affirms that someone like Elijah, namely John, would be a prophet of even greater importance.

The next episode is apparently a combination of a number of stories, put together by Mark in order to show Jesus' victory over the forces of evil. This miracle concludes the section begun by the first prediction of the passion. The disciples play a special role, especially at the end, but the miracle is addressed to the crowds, who even more than the disciples, are still missing the point of Jesus' message. As told here, the story is a prefigurement of Jesus' death and Resurrection (the boy became like a corpse), and an appeal for faith in Jesus. The disciples couldn't cast out the demon, probably because their usual method of doing so was by dialogue. The boy was a deaf-mute; therefore no dialogue was possible. They didn't know what to do. Jesus replies that they should pray. Perhaps their prayer was weak because their faith in Jesus was weak. In any case, this incident once again points up Jesus' superiority over the disciples.

The second prediction of the Passion and Resurrection is similar to the first. Mark repeats it in order to emphasize the significance of this teaching.

He then follows this second teaching with a long series of instructions on various topics; each saying is an incident describing some aspect of discipleship and commitment to the reign of God. In a sense, this section might be characterized as a "question and answer" period, compiled by Mark from the source material he has available. Its purpose is to instruct the disciples who still fail to understand the necessity of Jesus' suffering.

His instruction first emphasizes that the disciples are to serve others, and not be ambitious about their own prestige. Jesus then adopts a very tolerant attitude towards those who expel demons but who do not officially belong to the disciples of Jesus. Previously the scribes and Pharisees attacked Jesus by saying that he drives out demons by the power of the devil. Here the disciples are making the same accusation of someone else. The response of Jesus is consistent with his earlier reply to the Jewish leaders: Leave him alone, he's more with us than against us. Then Mark adds the important comment that helping people in seemingly little things like giving them a cup of water is a genuine act worthy of reward in the reign of God.

There follows immediately a series of sayings related to characteristics of a true follower of Jesus. Destroying the faith of others is directly opposed to the reign of God. Becoming ensnared in yourself, whether it's your hand, your foot, your eye, or any part of you leads a person away from Jesus. Living according to the reign of God comes first, and that style of life demands concern for others; to selfishly concentrate on your own desires, to the detriment of other people, is not the behavior of a dedicated disciple. Mark concludes this series with the appeal to perseverance, that is, remain "salted" even under trying conditions (like persecution). Don't give up. The final word is a promise of peace with one another if they live out the attitudes just described. This instruction began with the disciples arguing with each other about who was the best among them. After the instruction they should be at peace with one another.

The "question and answer period" continues. This time the question centers on divorce. Jesus' view on the indissolubility of marriage is a new teaching. He insists on it without compromise, and by doing so he establishes his own authority even above the authority of Moses. Once a man and woman have been truly joined, they cannot be truly separated.

The next episode about the little children may be a reference to the Jewish custom of bringing the children to a scribe before the feast of the Day of Atonement for a blessing. The disciples objected probably because they didn't want the parents to think of Jesus as "just a mere scribe." But Jesus uses the occasion for teaching a lesson: It is childlike confidence that makes it possible for a follower of Jesus to call God by his true title, that is, Father.

Jesus makes some strong statements about riches as well. The rich man comes to him asking a question, "How do I attain eternal life?" Jesus rebukes him a little, probably because the man wants an answer that would automatically assure him of eternal life. In effect, Jesus maintains that it's not that easy. The man's priorities are still not consistent with the reign of God: He follows the commandments but his riches still come first. Jesus says that God must come first. The man is saddened because he didn't expect that kind of a challenge and isn't ready to follow it. The strength of Jesus' teaching amazes and puzzles the disciples, particularly since the common Jewish thought was that riches were a sign of God's favor. The richer you were, the more God favored you. Jesus absolutely denies that principle. The bewilderment of the disciples is great, since Jesus' pronouncement was very severe. They therefore ask him about it, and he softens the teaching about riches by admitting that "with God" it is possible for a rich man to enter the reign of God. Peter then reminds Jesus that the disciples should be able to make it, since they are following him. Peter seems worried about living up to this difficult command of Jesus. Jesus in turn, reassures the disciples that there are rewards for following him. But it's interesting that in the midst of the list of rewards Mark adds a note about persecution as well. He keeps the theme of suffering in mind even when he promises happiness. This mention of suffering leads into the third prediction of the Passion and Resurrection.

The third prediction is basically the same as the previous two, but there is an added tone to this rendition. There's a feeling of immediacy present here: Jesus is on his way to Jerusalem where it's all going to happen. He's walking ahead of the disciples, seemingly impatient to fulfill his mission.

The disciples continue to miss the message. This time the focus is on James and John, who ask for a personal place of honor, for prestige in the coming reign of God. They seem to accept the fact that suffering will be part of their discipleship, and as such that's an improvement in their understanding. But they're concentrating on their reward and doing so in a spirit of competition with the other disciples. In effect, Jesus repeats a previous teaching: In the reign of God disciples must serve one another, not dispute about who's the best among them. Those in authority must be servants to others. It's a service that Jesus, as the Suffering Son of Man, will push to its completeness, by dying as an innocent victim for the sake of others.

The story about the disciples arguing over the places of honor is followed by the story of a blind beggar. The contrast is intended: the blind beggar seems to have the message of Jesus clearer than the disciples. Jesus asks him the same question he asked James and John: "What do you want?" The beggar replies that he wants to see— a request for service. The disciples answered that they wanted prestige—an attitude unacceptable in the reign of God. This story of Bartimaeus is also a prelude to the next episode in the gospel, Jesus' triumphant entry into Jerusalem. The repeated acclamation about the Son of David is a title of great honor, and Jesus accepts it. There is no longer the command to keep silence, since the end is so near anyway. Jesus commends the blind man for his faith, and like a true disciple the man begins to follow the Lord.

It's on that note of sight received and commitment to follow Jesus that this section of the gospel comes to an end. It is a fitting ending since throughout these chapters Jesus has been trying to make the disciples see the necessity for his suffering and has been challenging them to commit themselves to follow in his path.

Where Did This Message Come From?

Mark was a man of faith and that faith influenced the writing of his gospel. But he was also a man of his times. As such, he was in touch with the major political and social events of his age. It was a world controlled by the Romans politically and militarily, controlled rather well; there had not been a major war for a century. Besides, the Romans were wise and "good" conquerors. They certainly turned many people into slaves, but at the same time, they left many nations a remarkable degree of independence. Local governments formed and operated by the people of the conquered country had the authority to govern their people on most local political and religious matters. The Romans were there and were the final authority; they diligently kept their eyes on things. But they seriously tried not to interfere with most of the internal affairs of these smaller and weaker nations. The policy of Rome was to reserve to themselves two particular facets of political life: First, they exercised the right to collect taxes, and secondly, they made the final judgment regarding the death penalty.

Jesus and Mark lived under those social conditions. It was not the best of situations, but it was not the worst either. The Jewish people and leaders along with the early Christians had to respond to those conditions. Some Jewish leaders decided to go along with the Romans, to keep them happy and make the best out of the situation. Other Jews wanted to overthrow the Romans, to assume complete control of their country once again. This second group of Jews eventually engendered a deliberate, outright revolution against the Romans, and of course, the Romans grew impatient with these rebels and finally decided to put an end to their troublesome activities. In 70 A.D. Roman armies entered Israel and within a relatively short period of time, destroyed the nation, wiped out Jerusalem and the temple, and established a brand new country. From that time until 1948, the Jews never had a nation of their own; they were forced to live in non-Jewish countries. They banded together in ghettoes, attempting to preserve their religious and cultural values, but they were always "outsiders" in those countries.

These political events also affected the early Christian Church and they were part of the social background out of which Mark wrote his gospel. Immediately after the Resurrection, the followers of Jesus considered themselves and were viewed by others, the Romans included, as a sect or branch of Judaism. The disciples attended the Jewish synagogue, observed many of the Jewish practices, and accepted many of the Hebrew ways of thinking. In other words, they were Jews who followed the teaching of the Rabbi Jesus and who believed that this Rabbi rose from the dead. Indications are that many of the early Christians deliberately and joyfully wanted to maintain this very close connection with Judaism. Christianity did not emerge as a "brand new" religion; it evolved rather slowly out of the Jewish faith.

Two main events contributed to the eventual parting of the ways between Christianity and Judaism, one political, the other more "religious" in nature. Politically, when the Jews were losing favor with the Romans, climaxed by the Roman victory in 70 A.D., the Christians did not want to be associated with the Jewish defeat and persecution. Many Christians were willing to accept suffering and persecution, but not because they were considered Jews who were fighting the Romans. Being persecuted for Christ was different than being persecuted as a Jewish political revolutionary. As a result, the Christians generally insisted that they were not really Jews; they were something different. At the time, this approach seemed to work; for the most part the Christians were spared during this persecution. The Romans admitted a distinction between Christianity and Judaism; the followers of Jesus were no longer considered "just another Jewish sect." By 70 they were more than that.

The other situation which led eventually to a distinction between Judaism and Christianity was a more internal and religious problem. This situation revolved around the question of how to handle converts to Christianity who were not Jewish. We should not assume that the

Church in the first few decades after Jesus developed along the same lines in every city. In fact, quite the contrary seems to be the case. The Christian community in Jerusalem was considerably different from the community in Antioch or Corinth. Jerusalem was, quite naturally, the center for Judaeo-Christianity; the Christians there were practicing Jews before they converted to Christianity, and they strongly felt the need to maintain an explicit Jewish dimension to the new religion. In Antioch, however, there was a definite Gentile influence on the Christian community. They didn't see the need to be so closely identified with Jewish practices and ideas. It was inevitable that these two factions would clash.

The clash came to a head over the question of Jewish eating practices. The Jerusalem Christian community, led by James (not the apostle, but probably a cousin of Jesus), insisted that all converts, Gentiles included, must follow the Mosaic law about refraining from eating meat that had been sacrificed to pagan idols. Some Christians holding this position even went so far as to demand circumcision of all converts, which meant that every Christian must first become a Jew before he could be recognized as a true disciple of Jesus. The opposite position, held by St. Paul among others, denied the necessity of any of these Jewish practices. They felt that anyone who professed faith in Jesus could immediately be baptized, that is, accepted as full-fledged members of the Christian community. As a result, the Law of Moses about the eating of meat sacrificed to idols does not apply to Christians; salvation comes through Jesus, not Moses.

The climax of this conflict came at a meeting held in Jerusalem at which Paul was also present. Speeches were made: Peter presented his position, Paul had his turn and James offered a compromise. They all agreed to the general principle: the Gentiles did not have to follow the Jewish law in order to become Christian. But, rather inconsistently, they were told "to abstain from the meat sacrificed to idols, from blood, from the meat of strangled animals . . ." In other words, the meeting in Jerusalem reflected a significant division in the early Church and tried to resolve that division. The impression is that no one left the meeting completely happy with the outcome. What is important here, is the picture it gives us of the first decades of the Christian Church, decades in which Mark lived and situations which influenced the writing of his gospel.

As a result of this internal clash and the principle adopted at the meeting in Jerusalem (along with Paul's consistent application of that principle in his preaching and letter-writing), the distinction between Judaism and Christianity became more and more clarified. But the separation between these two religions did not happen overnight.

It was in the context of this struggle within the Church and of the social conditions of the times that Mark composed his gospel. He addressed himself to the Gentiles, and as such he "took sides" in the dispute outlined above. He agreed basically with St. Paul. In terms of the Roman occupation (his gospel was written before

the fall of Jerusalem and compiled probably in Rome itself), Mark was particularly non-political. He did not
"take sides" in that dispute, and apparently neither did
Jesus.

But Mark did not completely avoid his social situation either. When he makes deliberate reference to suffering for the sake of Jesus and for the gospel, he's concerned about persecution of Christians, either at the hands
of the Jewish leaders or coming from the Romans. This
whole section of the gospel, with its theme of the coming
Passion and Resurrection of Jesus and its insistence on
suffering, is a call to early Christians to be courageous
in the suffering they might undergo because of their
faith. Mark is reminding his readers that suffering might
be a part of discipleship, but that such suffering can
eventually bring joy, just like the suffering of Jesus led
to the joys of his Resurrection. And when Mark talks
about this suffering, he has in mind among other things,
the possibility of real persecution as well as the suffering
that comes from the divisions found within the Christian communities.

Mark's point is not that these painful situations will
go away, nor even that these "internal" and "external"
events are unnecessary. Mark's point rather is that the
suffering resulting from these situations can be turned
into joy, if Christians live up to the demands of true discipleship, if they follow the way of Jesus who was the
Suffering Messiah.

So What?

Pain has always been a part of life. Birth is generally painful, death is often the same, and in between pain is either at our doorstep or lurking around the corner. There's sickness and disabilities; there's the lonely pain of rejection, alienation, and unreturned and untried love. There's failure as well as the hidden pain of pride. Children cry when they feel it; adolescents sulk; adults become numb. Pain comes from within us, our deteriorating bodies and our confused, struggling spirits. Society causes pain, with its competition, its depersonalization, its short-sighted "remedies" and its false hopes. Pain comes to all men.

We take pills, have operations, and go to the doctor to ease the pain in our bodies. We become alcoholics, turn to drugs, and prostitute sex in order to escape the dreadful and unnamed pain in our disorganized spirits. We turn into ourselves and enjoy the devastation of self-pity, pulling others with us if we can. We cover up our inadequacies with superficial boasting, trying desperately to be accepted as we aren't. At times we project our inner pain onto others and blame them, and attack them in the vain hope that our pain will go away if we destroy others. Or we may desire pain, deliberately forcing it on ourselves, knowing that then we will have a good excuse for hating ourselves. Pain comes to all men, but all men have not handled it well.

Men have generally tended to avoid pain as much as possible. When it comes, it is usually tolerated, sometimes in a spirit of hostility, other times in quiet disgust. Pain comes to all men, but most men don't like it.

Jesus didn't like pain either, but he did something with pain that has been an inspiration to millions of people ever since. First of all, pain was not foreign to him. He identified with men in their physical ailments and climaxed that identification with his Passion and death. He also shared man's pain of loneliness; even his closest disciples misunderstood him and abandoned him. He struggled with the crowds, was a victim of their fickle desires. The leaders of his country were jealous of him, plotted against him, and finally eliminated him. The Roman governor was more concerned about his own ambition and in his cowardice condemned to death a man whom he knew to be innocent. And Jesus knew his own fate; he anticipated it, knowing the pain the course of events would cause him. He predicted what would happen to him, aware that death was the price he had to pay to continue his mission. Pain comes to all men, and it came to Jesus of Nazareth in large amounts.

What Jesus did with pain was to change it from pain to suffering. The two are not the same: pain is simple hurt; suffering is pain that is meaningful. To suffer means to elevate the hurt and to add to it the possibility of meaningful hope. To suffer means to create something larger than the hurt. In a hospital there was a man with a broken arm and a woman with leukemia. The man was bitter, angry and complaining about his broken arm. He experienced pain and he expressed pain. The woman

was pleasant, accepting her approaching death, and concerned about the welfare of her visitors. She experienced suffering and expressed suffering. The difference between the two is immeasurable, and very real. What a person does with pain is the crucial question, and Jesus demonstrated that suffering is possible, that there is more to life than death and more to pain than hurt.

Jesus made suffering and death the avenue to resurrection and joy. As such he accepted our humanity in all its dimensions, not avoiding man's fate, but offering man the hope and the faith that death is not the end. If death is the ultimate end, then all pain is ultimately meaningless—it is the final and complete evil, it is the inevitable victor. But if death is not the complete end, then personal and community hope is possible. And it's that message of hope that Jesus brought to man and Mark recorded in his gospel. That was why he tried to prepare his disciples by predicting his passion. That was why he didn't run away. He knew and he believed that pain, hurt, and death could not claim the final victory.

Christians are asked to believe the same thing. Do we?

CHAPTER EIGHT

Judgment in Jerusalem

Mark 11:1—12:44

CHAPTER 11

And when they drew near to Jerusalem, to Bethphage and Bethany, at the Mount of Olives, he sent two of his disciples, and said to them, "Go into the village opposite you, and immediately as you enter it you will find a colt tied, on which no one has ever sat; untie it and bring it. If any one says to you, 'Why are you doing this?' say, 'The Lord has need of it and will send it back here immediately.'" And they went away, and found a colt tied at the door out in the open street; and they untied it. ⁵And those who stood there said to them, "What are you doing, untying the colt?" And they told them what Jesus had said; and they let them go. And they brought the colt to Jesus, and threw their garments on it; and he sat upon it. And many spread their garments on the road, and others spread leafy branches which they had cut from the fields. And those who went before and those who followed cried out, "Hosanna! Blessed is he who comes in the name of the Lord! ¹⁰Blessed is the kingdom of our father David that is coming! Hosanna in the highest!"

And he entered Jerusalem, and went into the temple; and when he had looked round at everything, as it was already late, he went out to Bethany with the twelve.

On the following day, when they came from Bethany, he was hungry. And seeing in the distance a fig tree in leaf, he went to see if he could find anything on it. When he came to it, he found nothing but leaves, for it was not the season for figs. And he said to it, "May no one ever eat fruit from you again." And his disciples heard it.

[15]And they came to Jerusalem. And he entered the temple and began to drive out those who sold and those who bought in the temple, and he overturned the tables of the money-changers and the seats of those who sold pigeons; and he would not allow any one to carry anything through the temple. And he taught, and said to them, "Is it not written, 'My house shall be called a house of prayer for all the nations'? But you have made it a den of robbers." And the chief priests and the scribes heard it and sought a way to destroy him; for they feared him, because all the multitude was astonished at his teaching. And when evening came they went out of the city.

[20]As they passed by in the morning, they saw the fig tree withered away to its roots. And Peter remembered and said to him, "Master, look! The fig tree which you cursed has withered." And Jesus answered them, "Have faith in God. Truly, I say to you, whoever says to this mountain, 'Be taken up and cast into the sea,' and does not doubt in his heart, but believes that what he says will come to pass, it will be done for him. Therefore I tell you, whatever you ask in prayer, believe that you have received it, and it will be yours. [25]And whenever you stand praying, forgive, if you have anything against any one; so that your Father also who is in heaven may forgive you your trespasses."

And they came again to Jerusalem. And as he was walking in the temple, the chief priests and the scribes and the elders came to him, and they said to him, "By what authority are you doing these things, or who gave you this authority to do them?" Jesus said to them, "I will ask you a question; answer me, and I will tell you by what authority I do these things. [30]Was the baptism of John from heaven or from men? Answer me." And they argued with one another, "If we say, 'From heaven,' he will say, 'Why then did you not believe him?' But shall we say, 'From men'?" — they were afraid of the people, for all held that John was a real prophet. So they answered Jesus, "We do not know." And Jesus said to them, "Neither will I tell you by what authority I do these things."

CHAPTER 12

And he began to speak to them in parables. "A man planted a vineyard, and set a hedge around it, and dug a pit for the wine press, and built a tower, and let it out to tenants, and went into another country. When the time came, he sent a servant to the tenants, to get from them some of the fruit of the vineyard. And they took him and beat him, and sent him away empty-handed. Again he sent to them another servant, and they wounded him in the head, and treated him shamefully. [5]And he sent another, and him they killed; and so with many others, some they beat and some they killed. He had still one other, a beloved son; finally he sent him to them, saying, 'They will respect my son.' But those tenants said to one another, 'This is the heir; come, let us kill him, and the inheritance will be ours.' And they took him and killed him, and cast him out of the vineyard. What will the owner of the vineyard do? He will come and destroy the tenants, and give the vineyard to others. [10]Have you not read this scripture:

'The very stone which the builders rejected
has become the head of the corner;
this was the Lord's doing,
and it is marvelous in our eyes'?"

And they tried to arrest him, but feared the multitude,

for they perceived that he had told the parable against them; so they left him and went away.

And they sent to him some of the Pharisees and some of the Herodians, to entrap him in his talk. And they came and said to him, "Teacher, we know that you are true, and care for no man; for you do not regard the position of men, but truly teach the way of God. Is it lawful to pay taxes to Caesar, or not? [15]Should we pay them, or should we not?" But knowing their hypocrisy, he said to them, "Why put me to the test? Bring me a coin, and let me look at it." And they brought one. And he said to them, "Whose likeness and inscription is this?" They said to him, "Caesar's." Jesus said to them, "Render to Caesar the things that are Caesar's, and to God the things that are God's." And they were amazed at him.

And Sadducees came to him, who say that there is no resurrection; and they asked him a question, saying, "Teacher, Moses wrote for us that if a man's brother dies and leaves a wife, but leaves no child, the man must take the wife, and raise up children for his brother. [20]There were seven brothers; the first took a wife, and when he died left no children; and the second took her, and died, leaving no children; and the third likewise; and the seven left no children. Last of all the woman also died. In the resurrection whose wife will she be? For the seven had her as wife."

Jesus said to them, "Is not this why you are wrong, that you know neither the scriptures nor the power of God? [25]For when they rise from the dead, they neither marry nor are given in marriage, but are like angels in heaven. And as for the dead being raised, have you not read in the book of Moses, in the passage about the bush, how God said to him, 'I am the God of Abraham, and the God of Isaac, and the God of Jacob'? He is not God of the dead, but of the living; you are quite wrong."

And one of the scribes came up and heard them disputing with one another, and seeing that he answered them well, asked him, "Which commandment is the first of all?" Jesus answered, "The first is, 'Hear, O Israel: The Lord our God, the Lord is one; [30]and you shall love the Lord your God with all your heart, and with all your soul, and with all your mind, and with all your strength.' The second is this, 'You shall love your neighbor as yourself.' There is no other commandment greater than these." And the scribe said to him, "You are right, Teacher; you have truly said that he is one, and there is no other but he; and to love him with all the heart, and with all the understanding, and with all the strength, and to love one's neighbor as oneself, is much more than all whole burnt offerings and sacrifices." And when Jesus saw that he answered wisely, he said to him, "You are not far from the kingdom of God." And after that no one dared to ask him any question.

[35]And as Jesus taught in the temple, he said, "How can the scribes say that the Christ is the son of David? David himself, inspired by the Holy Spirit, declared,

'The Lord said to my Lord,
Sit at my right hand,
till I put thy enemies under thy feet.'

David himself calls him Lord; so how is he his son?" And the great throng heard him gladly.

And in his teaching he said, "Beware of the scribes, who like to go about in long robes, and to have salutations in the market places and the best seats in the synagogues and the places of honor at feasts, [40]who devour widows' houses and for a pretense make long prayers. They will receive the greater condemnation."

And he sat down opposite the treasury, and watched the multitude putting money into the treasury. Many rich people put in large sums. And a poor widow came, and put in two copper coins, which make a penny. And he called his disciples to him, and said to them, "Truly, I say to you, this poor widow has put in more than all those who are contributing to the treasury. For they all contributed out of their abundance; but she out of her poverty has put in everything she had, her whole living."

What's Happening Here?

Jesus arrives in Jerusalem—the first time he's been in that city, according to Mark. His arrival and his activities there are adapted to Mark's purpose and the development of his gospel. Jerusalem is the place of conflict and crucifixion. To read just Mark's gospel, one would get the impression that Jerusalem was a very evil city. The other evangelists treat the city much more favorably, probably because, once again, they are writing to a Jewish Christian audience, an audience that had strong emotional ties to Jerusalem. Not so for Mark or his Gentile readers. For him, Jerusalem is the setting for Jesus' seeming failure.

The structure of this section is compressed into a week's time, though there are some indications that the time was longer. The first part of Jesus' ministry in Jerusalem revolves around three events associated with his arrival in the city. The second part deals with five stories describing his controversy with Jewish leaders, and this section ends with a strong condemnation and judgment against the Pharisees. The situation becomes more and more critical, building to the events spelled out in the passion narrative.

Jesus enters the city triumphantly. But the acclamation of the crowd is not necessarily a profession that Jesus is the Messiah. Rather, the crowd is hailing the future reign of David's son. In other words, the cheering crowd recognizes Jesus as a prelude to some other king, at another time which they feel is near. And yet Jesus is claiming some Messiahship by this action. The contrast between Jesus' Messiah and the crowd's Messiah is still in evidence. But Jesus seeks to teach by his entry into Jerusalem. He is not a man of war. He is humble and lowly, riding on an ass. Those celebrating his arrival are probably a little puzzled, but perhaps they begin to get the message: Jesus is not the Messiah of their hopes, but he is still a Messiah.

Mark dramatizes this entry into Jerusalem by stressing the religious nature of the event rather than its political overtones. No doubt both themes were present in the original happening, but with the description of the detailed preparations for the arrival and the spreading of the garments and branches on the ground, the deliberate intent of Mark is to emphasize the religious significance of the event. The cry of "hosanna" also adds to the liturgical dimension of the entry, putting the political implications into the background.

The cursing of the fig tree seems an interruption to the account. Logically Jesus should go immediately to the temple to clear out the money-lenders. But Mark throws in these few verses about the tree. Jesus' action here seems unreasonable—after all, why curse a fig tree because it has no figs when it's not the season for figs. Obviously something else is intended, and when we become aware that the "tree" was an Old Testament symbol for the nation of Israel, we begin to get the idea of this passage. This is a parable, acted out by Jesus to demonstrate his judgment against

Israel for refusing to recognize the Messiah when he comes. Interpreted in this way this brief event fits well into Mark's overall theme in this part of his gospel.

It's impossible to really determine when Jesus cleansed the temple of the moneylenders. But in Mark's plan this is the right place for it. It's quite clear what Jesus is doing here: exercising his authority as Messiah to condemn the abuses of the Temple and to challenge it to return to the purity of intention and devotion for which it was originally built. The chief priests and scribes naturally objected and wanted to get rid of this meddlesome carpenter from the hill country of Galilee.

The next brief section returns to the theme of the withered fig tree and is immediately followed by an appeal to faith. Much of this seems to be Mark's editorial comments, dramatizing the effectiveness of faith and the power of God. But these verses do indicate that the Lord's prayer was familiar to the Church at the time of Mark.

Following the events of Jesus' entry into Jerusalem, the cursing of the fig tree and the cleansing of the temple, Mark continues to depict Jesus in conflict with the scribes and Pharisees. The struggle is mounting in intensity; the condemnations are stronger. Jesus becomes more and more fearless, and the Jewish leaders become more and more drastic in their designs to destroy him. Jesus walks right into the temple area, knowing that a confrontation was inevitable. The Jewish leaders quickly gathered and angrily put the big question to him: "Who do you think you are, doing all these things?" It's the right question really, but the intention of the leaders is to trap Jesus. So he, cleverly, turns the tables on them, exposing their real purpose. They're afraid of the crowds, who still admire John the Baptist. But if they admit that John was a true prophet, then they would be guilty because they refused to listen to John. Therefore they back down. Jesus replies that if they don't know who he is by now, and by what authority he preaches, they will never know.

Jesus then preaches, using a parable to get his point across. Based on an Old Testament text from the book of Isaiah, the parable recounts the story of the plight of an owner of a vineyard. The vineyard stands for Israel, the owner is God, the tenants are the religious leaders of Israel, the servants are the prophets, and the son, of course, is Jesus. In other words the fate the prophets met (most of them were killed or at least rejected by the leaders) is the same fate awaiting Jesus. The question is logical and inevitable: "What will that owner do?" He will judge and condemn those tenants; the vineyard will no longer be theirs to work. The message is clear: God will reject the Old Israel and establish a New Israel, a people who recognize Jesus as the true Messiah.

The Jewish leaders leave and plot their next move. They have been embarrassed and challenged, and realize they have to be very clever to trap Jesus. They decide to send two opposing groups to him, the Pharisees who are probably more tolerant of the Romans and the Herodians who object to the Roman occupation. They try to flatter

Jesus in an attempt to catch him off guard. They pose a problem to him, one which appears to be impossible to answer correctly. If he gives one answer, then the Pharisees will object; if he gives the other response, the Herodians will attack him. Armed with this strategy they approach Jesus. He sees through their flattery and dismisses it immediately. He pulls the rug out from under their whole plot by giving a response they haven't even thought about. They're left speechless and defeated once again.

But they immediately regroup and try yet another approach. The Sadducees now come forward and offer their services. They have a question which they figure Jesus could never answer. The problem of the resurrection of the body was a difficult one, and one on which the Jews themselves were divided. The Sadducees were opposed to belief in the resurrection, and the situation they presented to Jesus was designed to ridicule that belief and to show that the written law of Moses did not allow for the resurrection of the body. It was a trap question again. If Jesus sided with the Sadducees, then the Pharisees could discredit him. If he sided with the Pharisees, then the Sadducees could lead the public condemnation of him. In other words, the Jews are trying desperately to get some seemingly legal ground to launch their attack against Jesus. They cannot kill him outright because the Romans have the final word on the death penalty. They cannot assassinate him because the crowds are then likely to rebel and make Jesus a martyr. They must discredit Jesus to the crowds and at the same time establish a legal foundation for their appeal to Pilate for the death penalty. That's why they continually try to trap him. In this instance Jesus simply states that after death the kind of relationships we have here on earth will be different. Therefore their question about the resurrection of the body is immaterial. Besides, he adds, even Scripture says that God is a God of the living which includes Abraham and Jacob. Therefore, they must still be living, the implication being that the Old Testament indicates a belief in the resurrection. The Sadducees are also defeated in their verbal conflict with Jesus.

The next confrontation with a scribe is much more friendly in tone. It seems that at least one of the scribes is genuinely impressed with Jesus and asks a serious question, not to trap him, but simply to get an answer. One of the tasks of a scribe was to determine the most significant commands of the Old Testament and rank them in the order of importance. Naturally, this caused differences of opinion among the scribes. Jesus' contribution to this discussion was not unique in that he singled out the two commands to love God and love neighbor. But what is unique about Jesus' approach is that he combined these two commands, putting them side by side, as two parts of a single moral principle. Jesus praises the scribe who accepts Jesus' interpretation. The other Jewish leaders obviously don't like this teaching, but they're afraid to confront Jesus any more because he consistently outmaneuvers them, exposing their lack of real faith.

The controversy now switches. Instead of Jesus

answering the problems posed by the religious leaders, he now takes the initiative and raises a number of questions for them. Jesus is on the attack. He goes right to the heart of the problem, namely, the kind of Messiah they are expecting. It was commonly held that the Messiah would come from the tribe of David and be a king like David. Jesus maintains that being a blood descendant of David is not the important point. No, the Messiah would be much greater even than King David; in fact, he would be so great that he could be called by the title reserved for Yahweh, for God. And since he's greater than David, his reign can be different but greater than David's reign. The crowd enjoys this because the Pharisees can't answer.

The climax of this section comes as Jesus attacks the hypocrisy of his opponents. These men put on a good show and demand "respect" from those "less fortunate" than themselves. They view themselves as being in a superior position in the Jewish community. But Jesus condemns them for their pride, their hypocrisy, and their practice of confiscating the savings of widows in the form of a temple tax.

The mention of the widow inspires Mark to add one final story. The lot of widows in Jewish society was an extremely difficult one. Mark uses this incident to praise the "lowly" and to demonstrate the true spirit of almsgiving. In the context of this section of the gospel, it's also a condemnation of the Pharisees who have just been criticized for their show-off approach to religious practices. The real worth of an offering should be judged according to the sacrifice involved, not the amount given. Another implication of these few verses is that Jesus will soon offer himself as a sacrifice, seemingly a poor offering, but in reality a great sacrifice.

The stage is now set for the next dramatic act in Mark's gospel. After an interlude about the coming reign of God, the passion narrative unfolds. The opposing sides are clearly drawn. The forces of evil will soon make their final, all-out attack on Jesus. As always, he confronts them courageously.

Where Did This Message Come From?

Eventually it happens in almost every society. What may begin in unity will wind up in factions. Within a few generations, a country is formed, gaining its own identity and independence: its citizens are enthusiastic and basically unified. Then differences emerge, and if it is not a dictatorship, those differences surface in the form of various political parties, each claiming it has the "best plan" for the country. One test of the strength of a country is whether it can withstand the pressure generated by these various and conflicting ideas and programs. If not dealt with properly, these differences could tear a country to pieces either by civil war or by dictatorship. The original unity is lost or at least changed, and the society becomes a combination of many diverse smaller political and social units.

This social development took place in Israel, and by the time of Jesus the Jewish society consisted of many factions, not to mention the Romans who conquered and occupied the nation. That Roman presence was perhaps the most crucial element of Jewish social conditions. Not that the Romans were everywhere: no, actually, in terms of the total population, there weren't that many Romans living in Israel. And as we saw earlier, Roman policy was to allow its conquered nations a surprising degree of independence: the Jews maintained many of their political and religious practices unhindered by their conquerors. No, the presence of Rome in Jerusalem was crucial not because of any policy or practice; it was crucial simply because of the Jewish view of their own identity as a "religious" nation. The Romans not only violated their political lives, but they also and more importantly, tampered with Jewish religious beliefs.

Jewish society was a theocracy, that is, they made little or no distinction between politics and religion. Every phase of life in Israel was ruled by God. Government officials were representatives of God; that's why, at the time of Jesus, the High Priest had such great power, both political and religious. A violation of civil law was a sin against Yahweh, and the Law of Moses reigned supreme in government. To betray the country was to betray God. To be a "fallen-away" Jew was not only heresy but treason as well. The Romans, then, as the final political power in the land, were resented because their presence challenged the very fiber of the Jewish politico-religious society. It's no wonder that to a Jew the Romans were not just conquerors; they were heretics, destroyers, perpetual enemies.

Along with the Romans came the Greeks, if not actually in person, then certainly in their thought, culture, and philosophy. The Romans conquered the Greeks militarily, but in time the Greeks repayed the compliment by conquering the Romans culturally. Rome was strong on armies, law, roadbuilding, and governmental organization, but weak in philosophy, culture, art, theology, and a "graceful" style of life. The Greeks supplied these missing elements to such an extent that the "ideal man" in the Roman empire was more Greek than Roman. This Greek cultural influence, known as Hellenism, swept across the Empire, gaining new converts in every land to the "Greek way of thinking." It was inevitable that this Hellenism would clash head-on with Judaism.

At the time when Mark was written this clash was still being heard. The Jews were divided: some favored the Greek style and believed it could be incorporated within Judaism. Others strenuously objected, insisting that any compromise with the Hellenists was a sinful betrayal of the Law of Moses. This difference of opinion, plus the unresolved debate regarding the presence of the Romans (some Jews wanted to "appease" the Romans; others wanted to kill them), and a good number of other social and religious factors created a Jewish society that was highly complex. The first century A.D. found many factions within that society, oftentimes at odds with each other, and very near to civil war. That new religious sect, the Christians, only complicated matters more.

Reading the Gospels, we get glimpses of these factions and groups within Judaism. The Pharisees, the Sadducees, the scribes, the chief priests all make many appearances in all the gospels. Who are all these people, and what do they stand for? Let's take a look at some of them. It's important to remember however, that we're not dealing with different political parties here—at least not in the sense that Americans know political parties. Nor are they really different "religious sects," such as Catholics and Lutherans. More to the point would be to say that the following groups of people are like our categories of liberal and conservative. And yet, this type of classification is not completely satisfactory either. What we are referring to in these classifications are "schools of thought" or "philosophies of life" or "differing value systems." They are very real in that they affect almost every aspect of an individual's life, from his thoughts to his feelings and from the type of job he accepts to the people he socializes with. These categories may help to unravel some of the complexities of the Jewish society, a society which is so often reflected in the gospel of Mark.

We begin with the Sadducees. They were the aristocrats, the ruling class—the rich, arrogant, "jet-set" of Palestinian society. They were Hellenized, probably because they traveled more and were acquainted with foreign customs. Their view was international; they were familiar with the workings of the Roman Empire and the court life of the Emperor. Within Judaism the Sadducees were the official heads of organized religion. They carried out their rituals and ceremonies with great exactness and pride, but they accepted only the written Old Testament with a special emphasis on the first five books of Moses. This belief put them in opposition to the Pharisees who believed in the oral interpretations of the Scriptures as well as the written texts. A Sadducee would interpret the Law of Moses literally and exactly, with a strong concentration on the laws regarding ritual purification. Intellectually, they doubted many commonly-held Jewish beliefs: they denied the resurrection of the body, the existence of spirits other than Yahweh, and a life after death. Their God was not concerned about man. They had little contact with the people, and although they were the rulers, they were not the real leaders of the people. They were the High Priests, but they were rejected by the people because of their arrogance, their cooperation with the Romans, their wealth, and their acceptance of the Greek way of thinking.

Then there were the scribes. The scribes were teachers, and as such their influence on the masses of the people was great. They were held in great respect because they spent many years studying the Law, and the Jewish crowds felt that ALL knowledge was contained somewhere in Scripture. A scribe would study the Law for so long and with such intensity that he could recite from memory not only the written Bible, but an enormous amount of interpretations of that Law as well. Ordinarily a man would not be accepted as a true scribe until he was about thirty years old, and it's quite possible that Jesus delayed his public ministry until he was the acceptable age. A scribe was not necessarily a Pharisee, but many of them were. A scribe was a teacher of the Law, a Pharisee was a strict observer and follower of that Law. It was the duty of the scribes to keep the Law alive for the people, and generally they accomplished this task. They spelled out the demands of the Law in great detail, but they also knew the loopholes and felt no scruples about using those loopholes. Their concentration on the Law led them to believe in the absolute necessity of observing the letter of the Law. External conformity to the Law, regardless of what the inner spirit or motivation of the person might be, was the avenue for achieving salvation. It is precisely on this point that Jesus challenged the scribes.

A Pharisee was a follower of the Law as spelled out by the scribes. The Pharisees were a "hard-nosed" group: strictly Jewish and opposed to both the Romans and the Greek style of thought and life. They endured the Romans, offering them passive resistance, simply because they didn't know what else to do about it. To them, Hellenism was a terrible evil and should be eliminated from Judaism. The Pharisees were aloof and "snobbish" towards the people. This arrogance had its roots in the belief that the only true Jew was one who followed the precepts of the Law as exactly as the Pharisees did. And most of the people of the land could not or would not live according to those exacting regulations. The Pharisees then thought they were better than most men, and they apparently seldom hesitated to let people know how "good" they were. These Pharisees were extremely careful to fulfill all the rituals regarding temple worship. They also believed that all knowledge was contained in the Scriptures and in the accepted interpretations of the Old Testament. The Pharisees were respected for their "piety" and they worked hard to convert others. Some of them followed Jesus, but the impression we get is that most of the Pharisees were "legalists," performing external actions without too much internal devotion or intention. They were not a political party, but they were a powerful group, since they, along with the scribes, were considered the ideal Jews. They believed in the immortality of the soul, the resurrection of the body, the providence of God and the free will of men. These beliefs put them in direct opposition to the Sadducees.

A number of other groups can be identified within Jewish society. The Essenes, though not directly mentioned in the Gospels (some scholars speculate that John the Baptist may have been closely connected with this group), were a monastic-like community living in the desert near the Dead Sea. Their beliefs and life-style are described in the famous Dead Sea scrolls. In a sense, they were a radical fringe of society, practicing an austere life of total devotion to the Law of Moses and believing in the exclusive "favor" of God to the Jews. A group known as the Zealots, on the other hand, were politically active, even to the point of pursuing open revolution against the Romans. Barrabas was probably a Zealot. The Publicans worked for the Romans as tax-collectors and were generally despised by the people because many of them seemed to be corrupted by bribery and extortion. Then there were the "people of the land," the common people leading ordinary lives, without positions or political power. They were the farmers, the shepherds, the peasants. Some of them were further classified as the "poor," including the widows, the orphans, and those heavily in debt. The blind, the beggars, the bandits were labeled "the outcasts." A Samaritan was usually rejected by a Jew because Samaritans had mixed blood: they were the descendants of marriages between Jews and Gentiles.

A final word could be added about the "Diaspora." These were faithful Jews, about two and one half million of them, who lived outside of Palestine. They came from Alexandria, Rome, all the major cities of the Mediterranean Basin. These Jews kept close contact with Jerusalem. Their relationships to their "pagan" neighbors often seemed to be strained, even though these Diaspora Jews attempted to adapt themselves to their surroundings as much as they could. It was this group that translated the Old Testament from Hebrew into Greek, the most common language of the Roman Empire. It was also this group of Jews living outside of Israel that St. Paul visited and preached to when he made his missionary journeys.

Jewish society, then, was complex. The preceding classifications are simplifications—not every Pharisee, not every Sadducee, nor publican fits into these neat categories. But this overview of Jewish society at the time of Jesus and Mark can provide us with some helpful background information as we read about these various classes of people entering and leaving Mark's account of the life, death and resurrection of Jesus.

So What?

Prophets are needed in every age. The history of man has shown and is still showing that men need reminders of what their destiny can be, what their obligations to their fellow men are, and how they can most genuinely respond to the mystery of life. Put in the terms of Mark's gospel, men need help in their struggle with the forces of evil, the evil that they find within themselves and the evil they experience and contribute to in society at large.

In a biblical sense, a prophet is not someone who foretells the future. A prophet is primarily a spokesman for God, a man who speaks the will of God, addressing himself to the present situation. He's a man of today, dealing with today's problems. There is oftentimes an aspect of the future involved in his prophecy. But that aspect is secondary. That future-telling is either a warning or a promise: He warns his fellow man that if they continue in their injustice and hatred, they will eventually pay the price. On the other hand, the prophet promises that God will not completely abandon his people, that if they live up to their obligations to justice and charity, a new age, an age of peace and joy will come. It's in that sense that a prophet deals with the future. His primary

concern is always with the present; he is concerned with the future only insofar as it relates to the present. He speaks for God now.

A true Christian prophet is one whose message is consistent with authentic Christian tradition, a tradition which has its basis in the gospels, and in the message of Jesus. The preaching and the actions of a modern day prophet will necessarily be relevant to his times; it will be a message that's needed in order to remind man of his own greatness and to encourage a deeper belief in the presence of God and the brotherhood of man. But the prophet is not out to please anyone or gain popularity; the motive for his actions is not to win human respect and honor. Most likely, the true prophet will be rejected, criticized, condemned, and possibly killed. Being a prophet is no easy job.

It's generally the task of the prophet to criticize. He can usually be found going against the mainstream of society. When the majority of people think everything is going along just fine, the prophet will rise and unmercifully remind everyone of their personal failings and of the present evils in society. When the majority of people are very depressed, on the verge of despair, and convinced that there is no answer to their frustrations, the prophet will speak of the loving and merciful presence of God, of hope, and of joy. He preaches the unpopular message, not because he enjoys being contrary, but because he "has to." In fact, a true prophet rarely "enjoys" his task. He will usually feel the temptation to go along with the crowd, but he will overcome it in order to remain true to his mission.

Jesus was a prophet, particularly in his condemnation of the Pharisees. He "had to do it"; there was no way he could accomplish his mission without a run-in with the Jewish leaders. He confronted them in their own backyard. The temple was their den, their place of ultimate security. Here they were safe. But Jesus drove out their security along with the pigeons. He came to offer man a truer way to believe and a deeper appreciation of what it means to be a man. He came to free man from his own insecurities and to invite man to believe in himself, in his fellow man, in Jesus, and in God's continued presence. Preaching this message necessarily meant confronting those who could not accept it, who felt threatened by it, and who took direct action against him. Jesus is a prime example of a true prophet.

The prophetic aspect of Christianity continues to this day. Each genuine Christian in varying degrees shares in this prophetic role. But it seems that some men feel this need for prophecy more intensely than others. The Berrigan brothers have suffered much and have accepted that suffering because of their prophetic stance against war and personal violence. Their testimony is a reminder to the Christian community and the world at large that Jesus meant it when he said, "Blessed are the peacemakers." The true champions of the civil rights movements are modern prophets, and they are also, by the way, men and women of deep prayer. There are prophets in our midst today, or at least people who exercise a prophetic role.

In our own way we can all be prophets. We can speak out against the evils of our time, or we can offer hope to those who are discouraged. The opportunities are there; we simply need the faith and the conviction to face them.

CHAPTER NINE

Destruction and Promise

Mark 13:1-37

CHAPTER 13

And as he came out of the temple, one of his disciples said to him, "Look, Teacher, what wonderful stones and what wonderful buildings!" And Jesus said to him, "Do you see these great buildings? There will not be left here one stone upon another, that will not be thrown down."

And as he sat on the Mount of Olives opposite the temple, Peter and James and John and Andrew asked him privately, "Tell us, when will this be, and what will be the sign when these things are all to be accomplished?" [5]And Jesus began to say to them, "Take heed that no one leads you astray. Many will come in my name, saying, 'I am he!' and they will lead many astray. And when you hear of wars and rumors of wars, do not be alarmed; this must take place, but the end is not yet. For nation will rise against nation, and kingdom against kingdom; there will be earthquakes in various places, there will be famines; this is but the beginning of the birth pangs.

"But take heed to yourselves; for they will deliver you up to councils; and you will be beaten in synagogues; and you will stand before governors and kings for my sake, to bear testimony before them. [10]And the gospel must first be preached to all nations. And when they bring you to trial and deliver you up, do not be anxious beforehand what you are to say; but say whatever is given you in that hour, for it is not you who speak, but the Holy Spirit. And brother will deliver up brother to death, and the father his child, and children will rise against parents and have them put to death; and you will be hated by all for my name's sake. But he who endures to the end will be saved.

"But when you see the desolating sacrilege set up where it ought not to be (let the reader understand), then let those who are in Judea flee to the mountains; [15]let him who is on the housetop not go down, nor enter his house, to take anything away; and let him who is in the field not turn back to take his mantle. And alas for those who are with child and for those who give suck in those days! Pray that it may not happen in winter. For in those days there will be such tribulation as has not been from the beginning of the creation which God created until now, and never will be. [20]And if the Lord had not shortened the days, no human being would be saved; but for the sake of the elect, whom he chose, he shortened the days. And then if any one says to you, 'Look, here is the Christ!' or 'Look, there he is!' do not believe it. False Christs and false prophets will arise and show signs and wonders, to lead astray, if possible, the elect. But take heed; I have told you all things beforehand.

"But in those days, after that tribulation, the sun will be darkened, and the moon will not give its light, [25]and the stars will be falling from heaven, and the powers in the heavens will be shaken. And then they will see the Son of man coming in clouds with great power and glory. And then he will send out the angels, and gather his elect from the four winds, from the ends of the earth to the ends of heaven.

"From the fig tree learn its lesson: as soon as its branch becomes tender and puts forth its leaves, you know that summer is near. So also, when you see these things taking place, you know that he is near, at the very gates. [30]Truly, I say to you, this generation will not pass away before all these things take place. Heaven and earth will pass away, but my words will not pass away.

"But of that day or that hour no one knows, not even the angels in heaven, nor the Son, but only the Father. Take heed, watch; for you do not know when the time will come. It is like a man going on a journey, when he leaves home and puts his servants in charge, each with his work, and commands the doorkeeper to be on the watch. 35Watch therefore — for you do not know when the master of the house will come, in the evening, or at midnight, or at cockcrow, or in the morning — lest he come suddenly and find you asleep. And what I say to you I say to all: Watch."

What's Happening Here?

This section of the gospel of Mark may be the most difficult passage for the modern reader to appreciate. There's a style of writing here that's unfamiliar to many people in the twentieth century. Perhaps this style is something like a combination of poetry, science fiction, preaching, exhortation and prediction. Technically it's called the apocalyptic style, and needless to say, it was much more common at the time of Mark. Mark didn't use it very often, but he does employ it here. As a result, this passage is easily misinterpreted.

What may be helpful in reading this discourse of Jesus is to remember that there are two themes, two perspectives going on, usually at the same time. The one topic concerns the coming destruction of Jerusalem; the other theme deals with the second coming of Jesus, under the title of the Son of Man. These two predictions are interwoven: in one verse Mark may refer to the destruction of Jerusalem and in the very next verse switch to the Son of Man idea. And sometimes the author might put the two themes together. Our task will be to identify when he writes about Jerusalem and when he's referring to the second coming. In both instances Jesus is exhorting his disciples to be vigilant, to be on their guard, to be ready for both events.

These thirty-seven verses are mainly a speech by Jesus; it's one of the few times in the gospel that Mark records such a long, continuous discourse. Placed immediately before the passion narrative, this sermon of Jesus takes on considerable significance; it's meant as a farewell speech to his disciples, and it describes what Jesus means to the world as the Son of Man.

The opening comment by one of the disciples regarding the size of the temple sets the stage for this discourse. Later in the gospel, Jesus will be accused before the Jewish ruling body of planning to destroy the temple, an accusation which is a gross misinterpretation of Jesus' comment here. At the time of Jesus, the temple was still under construction and was completed just seven years before the Romans destroyed it. The prediction by Jesus was fulfilled in 70 A.D. This prediction then serves as a springboard for the rest of the discourse.

In verses three to eight, Jesus looks beyond the physical destruction of the temple to the signs preceding the coming of the Son of Man. The coming fate of the temple and the city of Jerusalem is not forgotten; it's still present in the background of these verses, but the focus concentrates on the broader vision about the future of mankind. Peter, James, John, and Andrew are the only disciples present; they were the first disciples called to follow Jesus, according to Mark. The mention of this detail suggests that this sermon was a very special one. When we compare this episode as recorded in Mark with Matthew's version of it, we see even more clearly that Jesus refers here to the second coming of Jesus rather than primarily to the destruction of Jerusalem. In the true apocalyptic style Jesus begins the discourse with a warning against panic and lack of vigilance. This style of writing always contains descriptions of distress—wars, persecution, earthquakes, famines, and floods are all common elements in an apocalyptic form of writing. Even though all these calamities will take place, the disciple should not lose faith or perserverance because the divine purpose is working itself out in all this dissension.

The discourse, in verses 9-13, centers on the Christian disciple and is an exhortation to remain firm in the faith. The Christians will be persecuted in the synagogues, that is, by the Jewish leaders and will be brought before governors and kings, that is, they will also be persecuted by the Gentiles. In these crises, Jesus assures his followers that they will not be alone, that the Spirit will be with them. By the time Mark wrote this gospel, it was certainly true that Christians were hated because of the name of Jesus. This brief section ends with the repeated appeal for vigilance.

The next nine verses concentrate on the coming destruction of the temple. Indications are that Mark wrote this gospel before the actual happening in 70 A.D., but that living in Rome as he probably did when he composed this text, he was more than likely aware of the political situation in Israel. The reference in verse fourteen to the "desolating sacrilege" is most accurately interpreted as an indication of a foreign army occupying the temple, particularly the inner sanctuary of the temple. To a Jew this occupation would be the worst desecration possible. Jesus says, in effect, that the Christian should not attempt to defend the city; he should flee immediately since the city will be destroyed anyway. The Lord (Yahweh) is in control of those events; he can shorten them. The point is that the Christian should not abandon faith in God even in those terrible times, for the Lord remains with them. But they should not be misled by false Messiahs, who probably will claim that they can lead the Jews in successfully defending the city. This passage about the destruction of the temple once again, in true apocalyptic fashion, ends on another note of warning: be on your guard!

The focus now switches to the coming of the Son of Man in glory. These verses (24-27) look beyond the physical destruction of the temple and describe the time of the final victory of God. The imagery here is almost entirely taken from the Old Testament. The time of this event is left open; there is no way to predict it accurately. The message here maintains that the Son of Man will act as judge, bringing calm after the calamities and order to the chaos. He will claim his kingdom and exercise his power as ruler. The description of the sun darkening and the stars falling need not be taken literally. The point is that the distress of this world, the forces of evil at work in the world will eventually be completely conquered regardless of how powerful and destructive they are. The forces of evil will not win; the Son of Man will be victorious.

The discourse ends with repeated exhortations to vigilance (verses 28-37). Mark in this closing passage refers to both the destruction of Jerusalem and the second coming of Jesus. Mark seems to think that both events will happen in the relatively near future. But he doesn't really know exactly, no one knows except the Father. In any case, the Christian is to be ready, regardless of when the second coming takes place. This appeal for proper preparation is made to all men, in all generations, and as such it's obviously an appeal which goes far beyond the warning regarding the coming destruction of the city and temple of Jerusalem.

Sifting through the apocalyptic language of this section as best we can, the modern reader discovers that Mark is recording two ideas: there will be destruction, there will be evil, but there is also the promise that the forces of good will be stronger and will prevail in the end. It's these two themes of destruction and promise which have been the background of the gospel since the opening prologue. Mark continues and expands these two interweaving themes in this section of apocalyptic gospel.

Where Did This Message Come From?

"The end of the world is near!" For thousands of years, Christians and non-Christians have shouted that warning to almost every generation. Occasionally we read about a group who firmly believes that by a specific date, this world of ours will reach its final end. At this stage in history, the majority of men look curiously upon such groups and move on; mankind on the whole simply doesn't believe those predictions.

But those warnings are interesting from a couple points of view. First of all, they indicate that some people in every age are convinced that this world is not permanent. The change that we experience constantly will eventually come to an end. Secondly, these predictions indicate that the question about the end of the world has never really been answered, at least in terms of when it's supposed to happen. Generally, most men object to these groups not because they're concerned about the final outcome of the world, nor because they present a definite position about that outcome. Men object because the predictions state a specific date regarding the completion of human history. If we eliminate that element of predicting a definite time for the end of the world, the Christian, and many non-Christians, could be more genuinely interested in the question of the future of mankind.

The gospel of Mark considered the future of mankind, but did not put a specific date on the time when this final event is to take place. Mark—and Jesus—felt that this future and final stage of history was very important. It's a dimension running throughout the gospel, but nowhere quite so apparent as in the section we just studied. Serious readers of the gospel have always grappled with this future dimension of the message of Jesus.

Since the nineteenth century this study of the future as depicted in the gospels has been called "eschatology." Eschatology means the study of the "last things." For a time this study concentrated on four topics: death, judgment, heaven, and hell. But from a scriptural point of view those four topics are not complete enough; eschatology means more than that. It's hard to define all that is included in a study of eschatology, but it is convenient to think of it from three aspects. It involves the future of the individual, of the community, and of the universe. All three phases are important and all three are interwoven; they affect each other. Perhaps we can say that eschatology, including the three aspects just mentioned, involves a belief that in Jesus human history ended one phase and begins a new, final age, an age that cannot radically be changed, but which takes time to achieve its absolute completion. There is, in other words, two dimensions to eschatology: the dimension initiated by Jesus of Nazareth and the dimension of the second coming of Jesus at which time what was begun and guaranteed by Jesus will find its complete fulfillment. The reign of God has really begun, but the extension of that reign in the personal, community, and universal life of everyone and everything will take time, even though the ultimate victory of Jesus has already been promised and even though the most important event in that victory, the death and resurrection of Jesus, has already been accomplished.

One of the problems with this study of the future of man is that oftentimes it is clouded with imagery that is misleading. Pictures of angels playing harps, devils with horns and long tails, heaven floating on a cloud, and hell scorching souls somewhere down in the core of the earth are all too common with many people. These images take on a reality that is not supported by the Scriptures. As a result, some people in rejecting these images, also reject the whole study of eschatology.

But to reject such a study is to eliminate an essential aspect of the gospel. It cannot be disputed that there is in fact a future dimension to the reign of God as depicted in the four gospels and in the writing of St. Paul. The early Church was very concerned about the parousia— the second coming of Jesus. Evidence shows that many in this primitive Christian community felt that this second coming was going to be relatively soon. This belief affected much of their life. When this parousia did not happen, they gradually became less and less enthused about it. In the course of the centuries this enthusiasm drifted so far away that for the most part, belief in and concern about the second coming of Jesus was ignored. And yet such an attitude violates the testimony of the New Testament. The early Church seems to have been confused about the second coming of Jesus. This confusion is reflected in the gospel of Mark. The Church, in other words, did not immediately reach a full understanding of what it was. That understanding is a constant, ongoing process, continuing in our own day as well. The New Testament does not have all the answers, but it does present the dimensions of the problem. The gospel of Mark, for example, reflects a tension between history and eschatology, between the here and now world and the future fulfillment of the promises of Jesus. The gospel implies both aspects: on the one hand, men should become involved in the world, bring to it the message and the spirit of Jesus, recognize the goodness of the world, and actively cooperate in establishing the reign of God. On the other hand, the gospel maintains that this reign is inevitable, that the final outcome is determined, that victory is assured. Putting these two aspects together is a difficult task, and the New Testament doesn't really join them completely; it simply insists on the truth of both statements. It reflects the life of the early Church and of the Church of all times: The Church has a mission to help fulfill the world and yet it knows that this fulfillment is not complete and final.

Mark, in the section of the gospel we just studied, deals with eschatology. He writes about it in the apocalyptic style, but it's nonetheless eschatological in nature. He predicts the future and complete triumph of Jesus, insisting that the forces of history which bring about something like the destruction of the city and temple of Jerusalem will not withstand the power and glory of the victorious Son of Man coming to claim his kingdom. Included in this belief is a view of history that was not too common at the time of Mark. Many people accepted the idea that history is an endless chain of events, leading nowhere in particular. Fate is what really determined the future of man, and man had little or no control over his own destiny. Some held to the idea that history was a constantly revolving circle, always repeating itself, but once again with no specific goal for mankind. In this system of thought the individual often felt despair since life was meaningless. The biblical notion, on the other hand, accepted a world that was governed with and for a specific purpose; it was going somewhere. God was involved in it, and as such he refused to let the destiny of man become meaningless. At each turn of history, God is somehow concerned and involved, and in the end the power of goodness will overcome the power of evil. Through eschatology Mark records this final victory.

But this view of the future must be balanced with the other view found in the gospel of Mark and in Jesus. Jesus was in the world and with people; he did not withdraw from events in order to simply wait patiently for the end of the world. The same is true for the Church and the reign of God. The early Christian community evidently took time before they realized that involvement was part of the message; they had a tendency to withdraw from world events. They changed as time went on, accepting that they, like Jesus, must also go to the people and engage in history.

Today the tendency might be to neglect the eschatological dimension of the gospel rather than the involvement in the world dimension. Both should be present in authentic Christianity: involvement in the world with the active hope that we have an obligation to cooperate in the destruction of those forces which hold back the arrival of the coming victory of Jesus.

So What?

It wasn't too long ago that Alvin Tofler wrote a

book called *Future Shock*. The book is a warning: the rate of change is proceeding so rapidly at this point in history that the majority of people are having a difficult time adjusting to it. As a result, these people are experiencing a sickness that Mr. Tofler named future shock. The changes, which Mr. Tofler supports, are taking place in almost every area of life, from scientific discoveries to the restructuring of organizations and institutions. To be able to cope with this wide range of changes he suggests that we look into the future and attempt to predict as accurately and as specifically as possible what that future holds for us. His point is that if we know what's coming, we might be able to adjust to it better when it gets here and we might be better equipped to control the direction of change. This strategy would minimize the danger of future shock.

In one sense, the eschatological message of the gospel of Mark fits in well with Mr. Tofler's suggestion about anticipating the future. Jesus predicted a specific event in the future of mankind; that event may be the most significant happening in the course of human and universal history, namely, the end of the world and of history. We can learn about the past and seek to understand the present, but as Christians we can do more. They can know and believe in a specific future event—the victory of good over evil, led by Jesus the Christ. For the Christian the end is not in doubt. The time of that end and the specific process which will bring it about is basically unknown, but the kind of finish is assured.

The significance of this future feature of Christianity can be seen from any number of points of view. It provides a basis for hope and an atmosphere for encouragement in our necessary work in the world. We have jobs to do, people to meet and love, problems to solve and mysteries to wonder at. When we reflect on our lives, what we do, what we get out of it, what we give to it, and why things and people are the way they are, we can add it all up and arrive at a rather frustrating conclusion. We might be tempted to believe that, all summed up, it really doesn't mean much at all. The world isn't really going anywhere, except maybe downhill. Our own personal lives are unsatisfying and in the final analysis, meaningless. What we do, we might conclude, doesn't make any difference because there's nothing to contribute to. Oh, we may want basically to get along with people simply because we have discovered that that's a better way to live. We want to be liked, accepted, and loved. But we do that for our own sake; there's nothing really that we can contribute to on a larger scale. If we conclude that the future of mankind ends in total destruction, then our efforts for peace, for love, for joy are all ultimately hopeless. If we figure that man's history just keeps going round and round, with destructive and constructive forces perpetually struggling with each other, then we could also say, "Well, what's the use?" If we decide to be indifferent to the future destiny of man, then we run the risk of attempting to isolate ourselves from the rest of mankind, denying our solidarity with other people. Any way we look at it, what we believe about the final outcome of mankind will probably, consciously or unconsciously, affect our attitudes and our approach to life. Our conviction or our lack of conviction about our future influences our present.

For the Christian following the direction of the gospel, a basis for hope lies in the belief that the world is heading somewhere, a future destiny centered on the ultimate triumph of good over evil. Peace, despite all our wars, will be the final victor; love, despite our hates, fears, and prejudices, will win out; joy, despite our frustrations and anxieties, will succeed; justice, despite our consistent patterns of injustice, will permeate the ultimate future society. A Christian believes that as he attempts to bring about these characteristics of the reign of God and of the best within man, he is cooperating with and contributing to the final victorious end of mankind. The end of the world is not a disaster for the Christian, it is the goal, not just for himself but for the whole of mankind and of nature itself. Such a positive goal can provide deep motivation and active inspiration to the Christian struggling with the very real problems of war, hatred, frustrations, and injustice.

Working for the end of the world will strike many people as being a very remote goal. They want something much more immediate. What about next year and ten or twenty years from now? What about tomorrow morning? The immediate programs we establish and the attitudes we adopt can be evaluated according to the final goal. Does the program we are involved with promote justice and peace? Do our attitudes and actions contribute to love and joy? If we can honestly answer "yes" to these very immediate and concrete questions about our daily lives, then we are also, in the long run, contributing to the growing extension of the reign of God and are consistent with the final victory of good over evil. But we must answer honestly—and to do that, we probably need the impressions of other people to help us evaluate our present behavior. It is generally more reliable to work and to evaluate our work and our attitudes in the context of a community of people.

Christians are people who live with a promise, and like any promise, it concerns our future. That promise has not yet been completely fulfilled, but it has already been made. A Christian believes in the promise, the final victory, and cooperates with its fulfillment.

CHAPTER TEN

The Passion Revisited

Mark 14:1—15:47

CHAPTER 14

It was now two days before the Passover and the feast
of Unleavened Bread. And the chief priests and the scribes
were seeking how to arrest him by stealth, and kill him; for
they said, "Not during the feast, lest there be a tumult of the
people."

And while he was at Bethany in the house of Simon the
leper, as he sat at table, a woman came with an alabaster flask
of ointment of pure nard, very costly, and she broke the flask
and poured it over his head. But there were some who said to
themselves indignantly, "Why was the ointment thus wasted?
[5]For this ointment might have been sold for more than three
hundred denarii, and given to the poor." And they reproached
her. But Jesus said, "Let her alone; why do you trouble her?
She has done a beautiful thing to me. For you always have the
poor with you, and whenever you will, you can do good to them;
but you will not always have me. She has done what she could;
she has anointed my body beforehand for burying. And truly,
I say to you, wherever the gospel is preached in the whole world,
what she has done will be told in memory of her."

[10]Then Judas Iscariot, who was one of the twelve, went to
the chief priests in order to betray him to them. And when they
heard it they were glad, and promised to give him money. And
he sought an opportunity to betray him.

And on the first day of Unleavened Bread, when they
sacrificed the passover lamb, his disciples said to him, "Where
will you have us go and prepare for you to eat the passover?"
And he sent two of his disciples, and said to them, "Go into

the city, and a man carrying a jar of water will meet you; follow him, and wherever he enters, say to the householder, 'The Teacher says, Where is my guest room, where I am to eat the passover with my disciples?' [15]And he will show you a large upper room furnished and ready; there prepare for us." And the disciples set out and went to the city, and found it as he had told them; and they prepared the passover.

And when it was evening he came with the twelve. And as they were at table eating, Jesus said, "Truly, I say to you, one of you will betray me, one who is eating with me." They began to be sorrowful, and to say to him one after another, "Is it I?" [20]He said to them, "It is one of the twelve, one who is dipping bread into the same dish with me. For the Son of man goes as it is written of him, but woe to that man by whom the Son of man is betrayed! It would have been better for that man if he had not been born."

And as they were eating, he took bread, and blessed, and broke it, and gave it to them, and said, "Take; this is my body." And he took a cup, and when he had given thanks he gave it to them, and they all drank of it. And he said to them, "This is my blood of the covenant, which is poured out for many. [25]Truly, I say to you, I shall not drink again of the fruit of the vine until that day when I drink it new in the kingdom of God."

And when they had sung a hymn, they went out to the Mount of Olives. And Jesus said to them, "You will all fall away; for it is written, 'I will strike the shepherd, and the sheep will be scattered.' But after I am raised up, I will go before you to Galilee." Peter said to him, "Even though they all fall away,

I will not." [30]And Jesus said to him, "Truly, I say to you, this very night, before the cock crows twice, you will deny me three times." But he said vehemently, "If I must die with you, I will not deny you." And they all said the same.

And they went to a place which was called Gethsemane; and he said to his disciples, "Sit here, while I pray." And he took with him Peter and James and John, and began to be greatly distressed and troubled. And he said to them, "My soul is very sorrowful, even to death; remain here, and watch." [35]And going a little farther, he fell on the ground and prayed that, if it were possible, the hour might pass from him. And he said, "Abba, Father, all things are possible to thee; remove this cup from me; yet not what I will, but what thou wilt." And he came and found them sleeping, and he said to Peter, "Simon, are you asleep? Could you not watch one hour? Watch and pray that you may not enter into temptation; the spirit indeed is willing, but the flesh is weak." And again he went away and prayed, saying the same words. [40]And again he came and found them sleeping, for their eyes were very heavy; and they did not know what to answer him. And he came the third time, and said to them, "Are you still sleeping and taking your rest? It is enough; the hour has come; the Son of man is betrayed into the hands of sinners. Rise, let us be going; see, my betrayer is at hand."

And immediately, while he was still speaking, Judas came, one of the twelve, and with him a crowd with swords and clubs, from the chief priests and the scribes and the elders. Now the betrayer had given them a sign, saying, "The one I shall kiss is the man; seize him and lead him away under guard." [45]And when he came, he went up to him at once, and said, "Master!" And he kissed him. And they laid hands on him and seized him. But one of those who stood by drew his sword, and struck the slave of the high priest and cut off his ear. And Jesus said to them, "Have you come out as against a robber, with swords and clubs to capture me? Day after day I was with you in the temple teaching, and you did not seize me. But let the scriptures be fulfilled." ⁵⁰And they all forsook him and fled.

And a young man followed him, with nothing but a linen cloth about his body; and they seized him, but he left the linen cloth and ran away naked.

And they led Jesus to the high priest; and all the chief priests and the elders and the scribes were assembled. And Peter had followed him at a distance, right into the courtyard of the high priest; and he was sitting with the guards, and warming himself at the fire. ⁵⁵Now the chief priests and the whole council sought testimony against Jesus to put him to death; but they found none. For many bore false witness against him, and their witness did not agree. And some stood up and bore false witness against him, saying, "We heard him say, 'I will destroy this temple that is made with hands, and in three days I will build another, not made with hands.'" Yet not even so did their testimony agree. ⁶⁰And the high priest stood up in the midst, and asked Jesus, "Have you no answer to make? What is it that these men testify against you?" But he was silent and made no answer. Again the high priest asked him, "Are you the Christ, the Son of the Blessed?" And Jesus said, "I am; and you will see the Son of man seated at the right hand of Power, and coming with the clouds of heaven." And

the high priest tore his garments, and said, "Why do we still
need witnesses? You have heard this blasphemy. What is your
decision?" And they all condemned him as deserving death.
⁶⁵And some began to spit on him, and to cover his face, and
to strike him, saying to him, "Prophesy!" And the guards received him with blows.

And as Peter was below in the courtyard, one of the maids
of the high priest came; and seeing Peter warming himself,
she looked at him, and said, "You also were with the Nazarene,
Jesus." But he denied it, saying, "I neither know nor understand what you mean." And he went out into the gateway. And
the maid saw him, and began again to say to the bystanders,
"This man is one of them." ⁷⁰But again he denied it. And after
a little while again the bystanders said to Peter, "Certainly
you are one of them; for you are a Galilean." But he began to
invoke a curse on himself and to swear, "I do not know this man
of whom you speak." And immediately the cock crowed a second
time. And Peter remembered how Jesus had said to him, "Before
the cock crows twice, you will deny me three times." And he
broke down and wept.

CHAPTER 15
And as soon as it was morning the chief priests, with the
elders and scribes, and the whole council held a consultation;
and they bound Jesus and led him away and delivered him to
Pilate. And Pilate asked him, "Are you the King of the Jews?"
And he answered him, "You have said so." And the chief priests
accused him of many things. And Pilate again asked him, "Have
you no answer to make? See how many charges they bring

against you." [5]But Jesus made no further answer, so that Pilate wondered.

Now at the feast he used to release for them one prisoner for whom they asked. And among the rebels in prison, who had committed murder in the insurrection, there was a man called Barabbas. And the crowd came up and began to ask Pilate to do as he was wont to do for them. And he answered them, "Do you want me to release for you the King of the Jews?" [10]For he perceived that it was out of envy that the chief priests had delivered him up. But the chief priests stirred up the crowd to have him release for them Barabbas instead. And Pilate again said to them, "Then what shall I do with the man whom you call the King of the Jews?" And they cried out again, "Crucify him." And Pilate said to them, "Why, what evil has he done?" But they shouted all the more, "Crucify him." [15]So Pilate, wishing to satisfy the crowd, released for them Barabbas; and having scourged Jesus, he delivered him to be crucified.

And the soldiers led him away inside the palace (that is, the praetorium); and they called together the whole battalion. And they clothed him in a purple cloak, and plaiting a crown of thorns they put it on him. And they began to salute him, "Hail, King of the Jews!" And they struck his head with a reed, and spat upon him, and they knelt down in homage to him. [20]And when they had mocked him, they stripped him of the purple cloak, and put his own clothes on him. And they led him out to crucify him.

And they compelled a passer-by, Simon of Cyrene, who was coming in from the country, the father of Alexander and Rufus, to carry his cross. And they brought him to the place called Golgotha (which means the place of a skull). And they offered him wine mingled with myrrh; but he did not take it. And they crucified him, and divided his garments among them, casting lots for them, to decide what each should take. [25]And it was the third hour, when they crucified him. And the inscription of the charge against him read, "The King of the Jews." And with him they crucified two robbers, one on his right and one on his left. And those who passed by derided him, wagging their heads, and saying, "Aha! You who would destroy the temple and build it in three days, [30]save yourself, and come down from the cross!" So also the chief priests mocked him to one another with the scribes, saying, "He saved others; he cannot save himself. Let the Christ, the King of Israel, come down now from the cross, that we may see and believe." Those who were crucified with him also reviled him.

And when the sixth hour had come, there was darkness over the whole land until the ninth hour. And at the ninth hour Jesus cried with a loud voice, "Eloi, Eloi, lama sabachthani?" which means, "My God, my God, why hast thou forsaken me?" [35]And some of the bystanders hearing it said, "Behold, he is calling Elijah." And one ran and, filling a sponge full of vinegar, put it on a reed and gave it to him to drink, saying, "Wait, let us see whether Elijah will come to take him down." And Jesus uttered a loud cry, and breathed his last. And the curtain of the temple was torn in two, from top to bottom. And when the centurion, who stood facing him, saw that he thus breathed his last, he said, "Truly this man was the Son of God!"

[40]There were also women looking on from afar, among whom were Mary Magdalene, and Mary the mother of James the

younger and of Joses, and Salome, who, when he was in Galilee, followed him, and ministered to him; and also many other women who came up with him to Jerusalem.

And when evening had come, since it was the day of Preparation, that is, the day before the sabbath, Joseph of Arimathea, a respected member of the council, who was also himself looking for the kingdom of God, took courage and went to Pilate, and asked for the body of Jesus. And Pilate wondered if he were already dead; and summoning the centurion, he asked him whether he was already dead. [45]And when he learned from the centurion that he was dead, he granted the body to Joseph. And he bought a linen shroud, and taking him down, wrapped him in the linen shroud, and laid him in a tomb which had been hewn out of the rock; and he rolled a stone against the door of the tomb. Mary Magdalene and Mary the mother of Joses saw where he was laid.

What's Happening Here?

The story of the Passion and death of Jesus is familiar to most Christians. They have heard it before. Hearing it again and again has been profitable to many people: they testify to the fact that although the account doesn't change, they do. As a result the same story means different things to them; it strikes them differently during various readings of the text. As a child, there's one reaction; as an adolescent, possibly another impression is made; then, as an adult, there's still another reaction. Other people hear it as a child and retain that "childish" impression for the rest of their lives. And then there are those who never really "hear" the passion story: They know and can repeat the basic information of the death of Jesus, but they don't know the message of the story. We will attempt here to restate the basic information and to interpret the message.

Mark's form of the Passion and death is probably closest to the actual happening. It's remarkable in its simplicity and in its disciplined desire to stick to the facts. There are scenes of great emotion, but those emotions are clearly and simply stated without elaborate detail. There is drama in the account, as there undoubtedly was in the event itself, but that drama is presented in a low-key fashion. This section is the climax of Mark's gospel, building particularly to the centurion's comment that "Truly this man was the Son of God!" But Mark immediately moves on, content that in that one short sentence he has adequately summarized what he has been trying to say since the beginning. Jesus is finally recognized publicly as the Messiah, but as a suffering Messiah. This account is not history as we generally understand it, since Mark includes a theological interpretation of the events he is describing. And yet he tells his story very simply.

The Passion narrative begins with a statement regarding the intention of the Jewish leaders to kill Jesus. They must be delicate however; Jesus is in town, but so are many other Jews, including many from Jesus' home territory of Galilee. The leaders are understandably worried about the reaction of these crowds.

The anointing at Bethany is somewhat of an interruption of the passion. But Mark justifies its presence here by interpreting the incident as an anointing for Jesus' burial. The comment about the "poor" is not a call to neglect the needs of those in poverty; it is rather a comment which emphasizes the brief life-span of Jesus. The woman is praised for recognizing this fact and for expressing her love.

The Passion narrative continues with Judas joining forces with the enemies of Jesus. They are happy since Judas could supply them with the information they needed: the time and place when Jesus would be alone with no large crowds around to defend him. Judas is one of the Twelve, a close associate of Jesus. His betrayal is therefore that much more horrifying.

The Last Supper is presented in three phases: the preparations for the Passover meal, the announcement of the betrayal, and the Eucharist. Jesus' last meal is the Passover celebration, an annual event dedicated to remembering the Jewish Exodus from Egypt and to provide a formal religious setting for living Jews to express their thanks to Yahweh and to rededicate themselves to the covenant originally made on Mount Sinai. The purpose of this meal in the life of Jesus is to show that Jesus identifies himself as a Passover, as one who goes through the process of death to achieve the freedom of new life. This meal is a perfect setting for Jesus to accomplish what he intends. He then simply announces the presence of a betrayer, the implication being that Judas then left and did not participate in the Eucharist which follows. The comment about the condemnation of the betrayer is probably added by Mark himself. There is no indication that the other disciples confronted Judas, or even that at this time, knew he was the one.

Mark, in recounting the Eucharist, formulated the incident for the purpose of inspiring Christian faith and worship. The formulation of the ceremony is liturgical. At the beginning of the main course Jesus blessed the bread and states that this bread is his body, that is, himself. Likewise later in the meal he took a cup of wine, most likely the third cup of the Passover meal. As with the bread, Jesus proclaims this cup of wine as his blood. It's a reference to the covenant made by Moses on Mt. Sinai, and since blood indicates the life of a person or an animal, the point here is that Jesus will "pour out" his life for others. That "pouring out" will be bloody when he dies on the cross; it is unbloody during this meal. Through these actions Jesus establishes a New Covenant, which is similar to the Sinai agreement but much more extensive, and which will be concluded at the Messianic banquet in the future final reign of God.

On the way to Gethsemane Jesus states his conclusion that the disciples will leave him during the coming crisis. This act of desertion follows the continual misunderstanding the disciples have exhibited throughout the gospel; it's no wonder that such misunderstanding could lead to such cowardice. Peter, characteristically, objects to Jesus' flat statement about his disbelief and desertion. Jesus tells them all to gather in Galilee when it's all over. That's the place he began his ministry, the scene of most of his work according to Mark, and is logically the place where the resurrected Jesus will make his appearance.

Arriving at the garden, Jesus wants some time alone to consider his coming crisis. He suffers the deep pain of decision-making. The psychological suffering that he undergoes in the garden seems to leave him once he firmly and resolutely accepts the cross; after this episode he seems calm and courageous throughout the physical suffering of the next day. The three disciples, Peter, James and John, are the same three who witnessed the transfiguration and the raising of Jairus' daughter. They had seen his glory and were amazed. They are now invited to be with him in his loneliness and suffering, but they don't support him. The distress Jesus feels is real and so painful that he wants to die; death would be a relief. But throughout this deep depression Jesus still addresses God as Father, which indicates his continued faith in the midst of his agony and his confidence in the Father even as the horror of his crucifixion almost overwhelms him. At the end he calmly faces his destiny alone. The repetition of this scene and the disciples' continued sleepiness highlights the tension and loneliness felt by Jesus.

Judas makes his appearance, still addressed ironically as one of the Twelve. His traitorous act is emphasized by his misuse of the embrace, an act which symbolizes friendship. It was dark in the garden, and the people sent to arrest Jesus apparently did not know who he was. Judas was needed to point out the right man. Jesus confronts them with logic, exposing their true motives. They didn't have the courage to arrest him when he was with them at the temple. The disciples slip off into the darkness, and Jesus is left alone.

Comparing the trial and crucifixion of Jesus as recorded in Mark with the same incidents as recounted in Luke and John presents difficulties. One of the questions raised is the element of time. When did this happen and when did that happen? There seems to have been two separate occasions when the Jewish leaders questioned Jesus. One at night when they brought him in, and another one later on in front of the whole Sanhedrin, or complete ruling body of Jewish leaders. More than likely the first session was with Annas and a few of the chief priests, something like a pre-trial hearing. But Mark is not very concerned about the details of the legal procedure. He apparently mixes questions of the one session with procedures from the second session. He combines the two into one trial. (There is serious doubt as to whether the whole trial of Jesus was legal, that is, in accordance with the rules of the Sanhedrin.) Luke's account of this part of the Passion narrative seems more logical. Mark feels that it really doesn't make much difference.

The Sanhedrin was seeking testimony against Jesus. This action was needed to establish some legal ground for asking Pilate for the death penalty. There were no prosecuting or defense attorneys in Jewish court procedures. Witnesses were simply brought forward and if two of them agreed, the case against the defendant was made. The defendant then could speak in his own defense. In Jesus' case the witnesses couldn't agree, and according to Mark they lied. The accusation about the destruction of the temple was a complete misunderstanding of Jesus' earlier comments. The high priest had to interrupt, another very unusual and possibly illegal action. Jesus' silence may have simply been the most obvious response to the lack of agreement among the witnesses. But the high priest is determined to convict Jesus; he asks him a question about his identity. That identity is precisely what Jesus has been trying to establish since the beginning of his ministry. He therefore responds. Only the king could be called the anointed one of Israel. Jesus explains his answer with allusions to the Old Testament, the net effect being that he identifies himself with the one who sits at the right hand of God and acts as judge in the reign of God. He shares in the glory of God.

The High Priest rents his garment, a sign of formal disapproval and judgment against the defendant. The charge is blasphemy, ordinarily punished by stoning. The agreement by the rest of the Sanhedrin implies that the whole nation of Israel was rejecting Jesus. They immediately begin to punish him.

The overall impression of this "trial" as recorded in Mark is that Jesus didn't have a chance.

Peter's denial probably took place during the night. The three-fold betrayal builds in intensity: at first he claims ignorance, then simple denial, and finally he denies Jesus with vehemence. The point is that when he betrays Jesus, he does it deliberately. But Mark is quick to report that he repents vehemently also.

The Sanhedrin now moves to Pilate, in order to get his permission to kill Jesus. Pilate asks Jesus if he is the king of the Jews. The emphasis in this interrogation is not on the religious dimension of the title of king; before Pilate Jesus is not accused of blasphemy. The stress here is on the political overtones connected with the title of king—politics was a concern of Pilate particularly if the possibility of rebellion was involved. The answer that Jesus gives is a little vague, but it probably amounts to an admission that he is king although he would phrase the question much differently.

The mention of Barabbas and the custom of releasing a prisoner at Passover time explains the presence of a crowd hostile to Jesus and dramatizes the embarrassing situation Pilate is in. The effect of the incident is to show the great responsibility of the chief priests for Jesus' crucifixion. The involvement of Pilate is not emphasized; he's described as trying to save Jesus. In the end however he gives in to the crowd, and his responsibility is clearly stated.

To the soldiers Jesus is just another prisoner, and they enjoy the cruelty of mocking him while they prepare the execution. Jesus suffers as "king."

The crucifixion is described in almost matter of fact terms, in a tone that seems impersonal. Simon, and his sons Alexander and Rufus, are possibly Christians known to the Gentile Church. It's quite likely that Jesus needed help carrying the cross, since he had just been scourged. Golgotha was a place probably named because it was a hill shaped like a skull. The exact spot is difficult to determine since the city of Jerusalem was destroyed in 70 A.D. and then again in 135 A.D. But it's not likely that all Christians of those times forgot the place of the crucifixion. Mark's account says simply, "They crucified him." The mention of the dividing of Jesus' clothing recalls Psalm 22 of the Old Testament. The penalty Jesus was finally accused of was claiming he was "King of the Jews." The inscription came from Pilate and emphasized the political overtones implied in the title.

Naturally the enemies of Jesus come and gloat over their victory. Mark doesn't dwell on it, but his message here includes an invitation to faith, to the belief that even though Jesus suffers this kind of ignominious death, he still retains the legitimate title of Messiah and Son of God. There is more to the Jesus event than what a person can see on Golgotha.

Darkness comes, fulfilling the Old Testament prophecy that the land will be dark when Yahweh appears. Jesus quotes a section of Psalm 22, a psalm which includes this passage of seeming despair but which in its totality is an expression of trust in God and of consolation in times of suffering. The crowd on the hill misunderstood the quote, even to the point of referring to Elijah. At the very end of his life Jesus cries out, possibly in pain; the death comes violently. Some commentators regard this cry as a shout of freedom in which Jesus delivers his life to the Father. The curtain in the sanctuary of the temple was torn in two: this detail signified the end of the Old Israel and the beginning of the new, a time when the death of Jesus is the avenue to reach the Father. In contrast with the Jews, a Gentile—a Roman army officer at that—expresses his belief in the identity of Jesus. What this soldier meant by "Son of God" is debatable; what Mark meant by it when he wrote the gospel is clearer. This statement is the climax of the gospel and attests to the divinity of Jesus.

The mention of the people present at the crucifixion is an anticipation of the next chapter, when some of these women will go to Jesus' tomb in order to anoint him for burial.

The account of the burial of Jesus is another way to confirm the fact that he died. This description is not very flattering to the disciples or even to Joseph. The burial is very hasty and the disciples don't even show up. Such treatment at the burial of a Jew is a great insult and a violation of one of their cherished customs and Laws. There is confusion too about what day of the week this is: Was it the Passover? Was it the Sabbath? If so, a pious Jew would probably hesitate to participate in any burial rite. In any case, this account of the burial of Jesus anticipated the next episode when the women will return to find the tomb empty.

On this note the passion narrative according to Mark is concluded.

Where Did This Message Come From?

The Passion narrative in all the gospels is the longest detailed account of any event in the life of Jesus. It's also the section which exhibits the most continued similarities among the four gospels. These striking similarities, as well as the occasions of dissimilarity, present the reader with a number of interesting questions.

Where did this Passion narrative come from? In fact, where did the various gospels come from? Are they all

the same? When are they different, and why? Why wasn't
the early Church content with just one account? Did the
gospel writers copy from each other? If so, how much
copying went on? If they borrowed from each other, which
one came first? And which gospel borrowed from which
gospel?

It would be helpful to approach these questions from
two different aspects. First, we will attempt an answer
that will consider the four gospels as a whole. Then we
will concentrate on the passion narrative. This two-fold
response is necessary because of the unique nature of the
story of the death of Jesus.

It is revealing to look at statistics when comparing
the gospels. The gospels of Matthew, Mark, and Luke
have many more similarities in content, in style, and in
development of the story of Jesus than does John's account. John stands almost alone in his approach to the
life of Jesus. Matthew, Mark and Luke are called the
"Synoptic" gospels because they can be placed in paral-
lel columns and compared with each other, at times incident by incident. Technically this type of comparison
is known as a "synopsis." On the whole these three gospels
record the same words and actions of Jesus. There are
differences also, but the similarities are very striking and
suggest that these three, in some form or another, relied
on each other.

This reliance becomes even more apparent when we
look at the number of verses in each of the three gospels

and discover how much of one gospel is repeated in the others. For example, the gospel of Mark contains approximately 677 verses. (There are slight variations in this numbering because some Scripture scholars dispute the authenticity of certain verses, and some people combine two verses into one.) Of these 677 verses of Mark, a mere 70 of them are found only in Mark. There are 350 to 370 verses common to all three gospels. Besides these hundreds of verses, Mark and Matthew also share an additional 170 to 180 verses. In Luke, besides the 350 to 370 verses held in common by all three writers, there are 50 more sentences that are shared with Mark. Luke and Matthew agree on another 230 verses. What it all comes down to is that in Mark, as we have seen, there are only 70 verses out of 677 which are uniquely his own. In Matthew, out of a total of 1070, there are 330 verses that only he records. And in Luke, approximately one-half, or 520 out of 1150 verses, are his own. To say that there must have been some kind of "borrowing" going on among these three writers is an understatement.

Many theories have been advanced trying to explain the relationship among the three gospels. Some people have suggested that prior to the writing of the gospels, there was a common oral tradition in the early Church. This preaching took solid form almost immediately after the resurrection and was repeated often. When the evangelists decided to write their gospels they each, independent of each other, drew on this early oral tradition. The differences in the gospels are due to the different styles of preaching. Most modern critics would agree with this theory up to a point. They accept the importance of the oral tradition, but they conclude that oral tradition alone does not sufficiently explain the similarities among the three gospels; there must have been some literary exchange as well.

A second theory has two forms to it. In one version, the gospel of Matthew is considered the first written gospel, and Mark composed his gospel with a copy of Matthew before him. A slight revision of this theory speculates that there must have been a preliminary gospel of Matthew written in Aramaic which has since been lost. Mark supposedly used that Aramaic version. In either case, the gospel of Matthew is considered the oldest and the one the other gospels borrowed from. This version of the second theory is not commonly held by scripture scholars today. What most of them accept is the view that the gospel of Mark actually came first. The dependence of Luke on Mark is generally accepted, but the extent of that dependence is disputed. Matthew's dependence on Mark can be substantiated but not nearly as conclusively as Luke's use of Mark. In this version of the second theory the primacy of the gospel of Mark is the main feature.

Many Scripture teachers believe that Mark came first, but also maintain that there were other non-scriptural sources that Mark, Matthew, and Luke used in composing their gospels. These scholars say that enough evidence has been found to establish the existence of a document they call "Q," which has since been lost. "Q" would have been a collection of sayings by and about

Jesus written in Greek. In this theory, Mark wrote his gospel almost from scratch, but Matthew and Luke used both Mark and "Q" as their sources. This group of scholars seems to eliminate oral tradition, contending that the dependence of one gospel on another is due solely to common written sources. For that reason, this theory seems to be somewhat lacking.

Perhaps the most acceptable theory is one which would combine the elements of the other theories. This theory would accept the influence of oral tradition on the formation of all the gospels but also admit of a literary influence. This approach maintains that besides "Q," there likewise existed various "pamphlets" about different aspects of the life of Jesus. For example, this theory speculates that there was a "pamphlet" describing the parables of Jesus. This written document was available to all three writers, perhaps with some variations in form but basically the same stories. Another written document available to all of them would be a Passion narrative. Mark is accepted as the oldest existent gospel, and Matthew and Luke are dependent on Mark. This multiple-document theory, including a developing oral tradition, is probably the best present explanation regarding the development of the gospels. We need to admit however that even this approach is not totally conclusive; the problem of the formation of the gospels has not been completely resolved. Perhaps it never will be.

It is important to have a reasonable explanation of this process if we are to understand the meaning of the gospels as best we can. Knowing where the material comes from will help the serious reader understand the text more accurately. The interdependence of Mark, Luke, and Matthew raises questions which must be dealt with.

With this background in mind we need to say just a word or two about the Passion narrative, particularly as it's presented in Mark's gospel. Although there are many similarities in all four accounts of the Passion, there remains some distinctive features about all of them. Perhaps this distinctiveness could be described as a difference in tone, rather than major differences in the events narrated. Luke's approach seems to invite the reader to "become" Peter or Simon of Cyrene, to identify with the weakness of Peter or the hope expressed by the good thief. Matthew and John seem to concentrate on motivating the reader to adore Jesus as the Son of God. Matthew wants us to learn more and more about the details of the crucifixion. John never lets us forget that the Passion event is really a marvelous victory; Jesus is the "Lord of salvation," and the story revolves around the glorification of Christ. Mark invites the reader to look on at a distance in sorrow; his description is stark in its reality. The crucifixion in his eyes is the dark passage through which the Messiah must travel before he is glorified; the loneliness of Jesus is highlighted. All four gospels stress the innocence of Jesus, and each quotes from the Old Testament in order to show that Jesus was the true fulfillment of Israel's expectations. Even in this Passion narrative, the section which manifests the greatest agreement among the four evangelists, there remains some differences.

The form of the Passion narrative was also affected by its liturgical use in the early Church. Apparently, a passion account was recited in the Christian worship services, even before it was written in gospel form. This liturgical usage probably contributed to establishing a rather set, solemn, and stylized version of the Passion experience. Most likely, the evangelists were familiar with this liturgical version of the death of Jesus as they wrote their own accounts.

The gospels are complicated masterpieces of literature. The record of Jesus' suffering and death is one example of that literary genius. And for the believer, these gospels are also the word of God, a divine message shining through and working within the written message presented by the four evangelists.

So What?

Who is responsible for Jesus' death and does it make any difference? Why even ask the question in the twentieth century? Perhaps historians or Scripture scholars would be interested in the details of the death of Jesus, but that's their job. Who really cares, when it comes to their personal, practical lives? The story of the life and death of Jesus might be intriguing, as a saga of a man who courageously lived up to his convictions. But there have been many such men in history, and they have inspired multitudes of followers. What's actually unique about Jesus? He died a martyr—so did many others. Besides, he met his fate so long ago that his contact with today seems very difficult to establish. Spanning two thousand years is a task unfamiliar and distasteful to many modern men. Why not just leave Jesus to the past and look for our inspirational leaders among our own generation?

These questions are serious ones and difficult to respond to. Perhaps the basic question is: What is the relevancy of Jesus and of the gospels? A response to that inquiry will be colored by the faith or lack of faith an individual professes. Some people will find the gospels extremely relevant; others will find them basically meaningless. Even among believers there will be different reactions: Some believers will continually discover encouragement in the gospels; others will express their conviction that they know and believe in the basic gospel message and ask to move on to other topics. In any case the relevancy of the gospels is an important issue.

One way to focus the question is to concentrate on the death of Jesus. His crucifixion is probably the most crucial event in his life, as it probably is with all of us. And yet the issue remains: What does his death have to do with us?

Christian history has made many comments on that question. Perhaps most of these observations would agree that the death of Jesus says something about our own life and death. It says that Jesus, who claimed to be connected with all of us, was also connected with God. He shared our humanity with us; he was completely human, a man like us in all things except sin. He did not masquerade as human; he was not "faking it." Jesus *was* a man. That's the testimony of the New Testament; that's the clear and continual pronouncement of Christian Churches throughout the ages. At different times in our history, people have acted as though Jesus was not completely human: They emphasized his divinity by taking away his humanity. They insulted Jesus by making him a non-human; they destroyed the depth of his involvement in the world by denying him true existence as a complete man. As a result these people lost their real contact with Jesus the man. Other people have eliminated the divinity of Jesus. They have admired him, but they have taken away from him his special connection with God. To these people Jesus can do no more than any "good man" could do. He could show man a way of life, but he could not radically reconcile man to God. Basically we are left to ourselves, with no possibility of leaping the hurdle of our own weaknesses and tendencies to contribute to the evil around us.

The uniqueness of Jesus of Nazareth is that he is both man and God, with neither of those existences eliminating or taking away from the other. Other religious leaders, Buddha, Mohammed, Moses, Confucius, all offered a way to live life religiously, and there are basic similarities among these religions. Christianity also shares in many of these common elements. But Jesus differs from other leaders of major religions in that he, and he alone, claims to be God.

The Passion and death of Jesus dramatizes the humanity of the preacher from Nazareth. He suffered and he died like all men suffer and die. Who killed him can be viewed from at least two perspectives. We could point to the historical events and pick out the chief priests, the Sanhedrin, Judas, Pilate, the disciples and a whole series of people living at the time of Jesus, and say "They killed him." And from that one perspective that statement would be true. But that's not the point of the passion of Jesus. The gospel of Mark, for example, looks beyond those forces of history and views the death of Jesus from a very different perspective. Mark sees the passion event as a struggle between good and evil; it's the same theme that runs throughout the gospel. This is the primary point of view; the actual historical events are merely the stage on which this struggle takes place. In that sense, the struggle could have taken place at any time, in any situation, because every time and every situation has the ingredients of good and evil vying with each other for supremacy. The passion account dramatizes the very real presence and strength of evil forces within the human situation. And it expresses the completeness of the humanity of Jesus.

Looking beyond the historical events of Jesus' death, a Christian sees that in a certain but real sense he himself is responsible for the death of Jesus. Viewed from that second perspective mentioned above, it becomes clear how every man participates in the responsibility for the death of Jesus. We were not there driving in the nails, and those kinds of images can be misleading and harmful. And it's not really a question of what we would have done if we were living at the time and place of Jesus. More to the point is the observation that we can at times do very real harm to the people and events around us. In so doing we contribute to the forces of evil, the same forces which crucified Jesus. In that sense we were there on Golgotha when Jesus died.

Implied in this understanding is the conviction that man has the power to do evil. He can do evil unconsciously—a man can accidentally shoot a friend while hunting. He can do evil and not be morally responsible—an insane person could shoot someone. And he can do evil and be responsible for the act in so far as it is freely made—a sane person can deliberately choose to shoot someone. It is particularly this last kind of situation to which we refer when we say that man has the power to do evil, although the other two cases are also implicated. In psychological terms, this power means that we can give vent to deliberately harmful and destructive forms of behavior. In theology, this power means that we are sinners.

Accepting our own sinfulness is generally a distasteful task. We need to be careful here; misinterpretation is quite possible. Over the centuries, there have been many explanations regarding the nature of sin: What is a sin? What isn't a sin? What do we mean by sin? Without entering into this debate, it is possible to say that regardless of an individual's definition of sin, the core of the idea is an admission that man can do some form of evil. If this admission is not made, then much of the Jesus message is meaningless. Jesus confronts the evil not only in the world outside of ourselves but also the evil within us. If we do not accept that we can do evil ourselves, then we do not allow the message of Jesus to get "inside us."

This admission of our power for harm is not a statement which implies that we are totally bad. Quite the contrary. We are basically good according to this position, and we have the wonderful power to do good. Put simply, we're OK. But we are a mixture of positive and negative forces, forces that we put into practice through our actions, our values, and our attitudes. Observation of our own behavior and of the behavior of others leads us to conclude that we have both powers flowing from the same person. Admitting that we are sinners is a confession that we have and exercise the negative forces within us.

The Passion of Jesus assures us that he was completely with us. He was victim of the self-same tendencies we can all too easily identify in ourselves and others: ambition, pride, defensiveness, and an inflexible desire to hold onto a position. Since he was one of us, Jesus could take us with him. What he did, he could do for and with us. As victim of the evil in the world, he could take the effects of that evil—death—and transform it into good—a new, resurrected life. Jesus is not just part of the past: His message of the sinfulness of man and the redemption of man will continue as long as man himself continues. He does something with our sinfulness: He offers us the opportunity to be accepted and forgiven, and demonstrates that even at its worst man's cruelty can be conquered. He conquered evil, not by escaping it, but by facing it. If Jesus was God as he claimed to be, then he was in a unique position to deal radically with man's sinfulness. To a Christian, that's precisely what he did. He invites us to believe in his claim, to admit our sinfulness, to accept forgiveness, and to humbly proclaim his message to others.

CHAPTER ELEVEN

Death Destroyed

Mark 16:1-20

CHAPTER 16

And when the sabbath was past, Mary Magdalene, and Mary the mother of James, and Salome, brought spices, so that they might go and anoint him. And very early on the first day of the week they went to the tomb when the sun had risen. And they were saying to one another, "Who will roll away the stone for us from the door of the tomb?" And looking up, they saw that the stone was rolled back—it was very large. [5]And entering the tomb, they saw a young man sitting on the right side, dressed in a white robe; and they were amazed. And he said to them, "Do not be amazed; you seek Jesus of Nazareth, who was crucified. He has risen, he is not here; see the place where they laid him. But go, tell his disciples and Peter that he is going before you to Galilee; there you will see him, as he told you." And they went out and fled from the tomb; for trembling and astonishment had come upon them; and they said nothing to any one, for they were afraid.

Now when he rose early on the first day of the week, he appeared first to Mary Magdalene, from whom he had cast out seven demons. [10]She went out and told those who had been with him, as they mourned and wept. But when they heard that he was alive and had been seen by her, they would not believe it.

After this he appeared in another form to two of them, as they were walking into the country. And they went back and told the rest, but they did not believe them.

Afterward he appeared to the eleven themselves as they

sat at table; and he upbraided them for their unbelief and hardness of heart, because they had not believed those who saw him after he had risen. [15]And he said to them, "Go into all the world and preach the gospel to the whole creation. He who believes and is baptized will be saved; but he who does not believe will be condemned. And these signs will accompany those who believe: in my name they will cast out demons; they will speak in new tongues; they will pick up serpents, and if they drink any deadly thing, it will not hurt them; they will lay their hands on the sick, and they will recover."

So then the Lord Jesus, after he had spoken to them, was taken up into heaven, and sat down at the right hand of God. [20]And they went forth and preached everywhere, while the Lord worked with them and confirmed the message by the signs that attended it. Amen.

What's Happening Here?

The tomb is empty. Three women discover this un-expected situation when they go to anoint Jesus. They are told to spread the word to the disciples who are to meet Jesus in Galilee. But the women become frightened and they don't tell anyone.

Thus ends the gospel according to Mark. It's an abrupt ending, so abrupt that many people believe that the complete ending of Mark's gospel has been lost. Verses one to eight in this final chapter are the work of Mark himself, but verses nine to twenty were added by someone else at a later time. The vocabulary and the style of writing used in this last section indicate that the composer of these last eleven verses was not Mark. Who this author was we don't know, but the date of composition was some-time in the first or second century. This passage is ac-cepted however as a truly inspired part of the gospel.

The precision and detail of the Passion narrative evap-orate when it comes to the various accounts of the resurrec-tion. None of the evangelists record the actual rising; they concentrate on two related themes: the discovery of the empty tomb and the appearances of Jesus after his death. Compared with the story of the death of Jesus, this ap-proach to the resurrection may seem surprising. The Resurrection and the Ascension are the crowning events of his life—the unique, astounding experience of life after death made visible to his disciples. One would expect precision and detail in recording this Resurrection event.

But it's not there. Apparently the early Church felt no need for one coordinated Resurrection account, although they felt a need for a coordinated Passion account.

The women went to the tomb obviously to honor the dead. They delayed their arrival there not because they couldn't anoint a corpse on the Sabbath, but because they couldn't buy the spices on the Sabbath. According to Mark, a Resurrection had not even entered their minds; they didn't even consider the stone that would be in their way. The point is that they didn't believe in the possibility of Jesus' Resurrection. They accepted his death as final—and perhaps as failure.

In Mark's view, the young man sitting there was like an Old Testament "angel," a messenger from God. What the author is trying to convey is not just that the tomb was empty; rather the concentration is on how the women are to interpret that empty tomb. What does the empty tomb mean? What it means is that "Jesus has been raised up. Go, tell the disciples to meet him in Galilee." It's interesting to note that, although Peter and the disciples get special mention in this passage, it's the women who are the first beneficiaries of the Resurrection message. The women are silenced by the mystery. Why they said nothing, we do not know. Mark undoubtedly had a purpose in recording it this way. But this is his last verse; the rest may have been lost. Perhaps the next lost passage would have clarified Mark's purpose here. Maybe he was returning to the theme of the "Messianic secret" for a minute. Maybe he wanted to de-emphasize the role the women played in spreading the news about the Resurrection. Whatever the reason, this verse as it stands now is a strange ending to his gospel.

This strangeness must have been felt by the early Church as well. Their tradition had more to say about the resurrection of Jesus. Consequently, someone composed these final eleven verses in order to clarify their belief in the Resurrection.

The emphasis in the appearances recorded in this longer ending underlines the disbelief of the disciples. They had lost their Master, and they were sad and disappointed. This account is not too flattering to the disciples, since they continue to be unbelieving until the Lord himself comes to them "at table." Jesus rebukes them for their stubbornness, much like he did throughout the gospel.

This ending of the gospel concludes on a note of universalism—go to the whole world and proclaim the good news. Faith and baptism are the conditions for salvation. In other words, men of all times will have to take a stand regarding the event and message of Jesus. The signs described here are indications that the reign of God has been established. Much of this terminology is from the Old Testament, and it does not mean that these are the only signs of the reign of God.

The conclusion to this section is the Ascension which, according to this author, takes place on Easter itself. The crucified Jesus is exalted and honored by his Father.

In verse twenty, the author calls him "Lord," a title of supreme respect. It is this Lord who works with the disciples in their proclamation of the good news and who is present in the message they preach particularly through the signs that accompany this proclamation.

It is on this note of proclamation that Mark began his gospel, and it is on this note that this composition ends. In between, the reader witnessed conflict, struggle, misunderstanding, joy, faith, frustration, loyalty, disbelief, passion, death, resurrection, and ascension. The final proclamation and all that went before it—every episode, every story, every event in some way or another described what Mark meant in chapter 1, verse fifteen: "This is the time of fulfillment. The reign of God is at hand! Reform your lives and believe in the gospel!"

Where Did This Message Come From?

Anyway a person looks at it, the claim that Jesus rose from the dead is crucial to Christianity. Without it, we have a dead Jesus and disbelieving, confused, frightened, and frustrated disciples. With it, we have the culmination of the gospel of Mark, the final victory in the continuous struggle presented by the author. With it, we have a living Jesus and dedicated, committed, faithful, and confident disciples. With it, we have a major ingredient in the formation of the early Christian community. Without it, we have fraud, deceit, lying, and/or emotional instability, hallucinations, and "visions" by disturbed people. Without it, we have either a gigantic, planned hoax engendered by the followers of Jesus, or we are dealing with an early Church all of the members of which are crazy. In any case, the Resurrection, and the meaning of the Resurrection, is crucial to Christianity.

Christianity, of course, insists on the fact of the Resurrection. The empty tomb made a difference to the first followers of Jesus; they did not ignore that Easter event. The proclamation of the death, Resurrection and Ascension of Jesus was the core of their preaching and the basis of their motivation.

The Biblical evidence of these astounding events is confusing. The passion narrative is precise and detailed, and the four gospel writers generally agree in their description of the death of Jesus. But the Resurrection and Ascension accounts vary greatly. One explanation for this seeming lack of agreement among the four evangelists takes us back to the conditions and problems the early Church had to face. For them a major difficulty in preaching about Jesus was to convince the listeners that Jesus was not a common criminal. After all, a listener could reason, Jesus was crucified—the fate of criminals. The first preachers had to demonstrate the innocence of the man crucified. Though he died like a criminal, he was not a criminal. As a result, they developed the long Passion narrative very early in the life of the Church in order to meet the objections of possible converts to Christianity. The tradition about the death of Jesus became established in a relative set form even before the evangelists composed their gospels.

But when it came to the event of the resurrection these early preachers did not meet the same kind of reaction. This is not to say that everyone immediately believed in the Resurrection; it is simply to say that there was no need to develop the same precision in the telling of the event. They had to "prove" that Jesus was not a criminal. They could only state that Jesus was risen from the dead: The tomb was empty and they saw him after he had risen. Descriptions of who had seen him first under what conditions, or of how the tomb became empty are not the main points at all. The authors felt free to arrange those descriptions according to their own theological and literary purposes. The important points were to proclaim the empty tomb and to insist that it was really Jesus who was seen. Once those themes are clarified, the listener or reader could either believe or disbelieve.

Consequently, the Resurrection tradition consists of isolated appearances of Jesus with very little agreement among the various gospel accounts regarding details. One example of this disagreement emerges when we ask: Where did these appearances take place? According to Luke, in John chapter 20, and Mark chapter 16 verses 9-20, the appearances took place in Jerusalem. But in Matthew, in John chapter 21, and in Mark chapter 16 verses 1-8, Jesus appeared to the disciples in Galilee. And it's not sufficient to say that Jesus appeared in both places, and therefore there would be no real disagreement among these various traditions. No, the Jerusalem accounts leave no room for another appearance in Galilee. Besides, in Luke and in Mark 16:9-20, the Ascension, the departure of Jesus, is described as taking place on Easter night. Even if the risen Jesus could appear in Jerusalem and in Galilee on the same day as his resurrection, it's certainly true that the disciples couldn't get from one place to the other that fast. Once again, the Galilean accounts seem to rule out any prior experience of the risen Lord, whether in Jerusalem or anywhere. In Matthew the disciples doubt the appearance in Galilee. If they had witnessed a resurrected Lord in Jerusalem, they had no cause for doubt for seeing him in Galilee. And it's apparent from the story in Mark and in Matthew that the disciples are seeing Jesus for the first time since his death.

Some people have tried mightily to arrange these events, these appearances, these indications of the time and place into some unified, continuous story. But such attempts at unification only lead to failure; it cannot be done while remaining true to all the biblical evidence. Each gospel has its own story to tell in its own way; each recounts an important appearance of the resurrected Jesus, but every account is different in its details. This central appearance is highlighted in each account with the commission to the disciples to preach the gospel to all the nations. Perhaps there was one appearance of the risen Lord, and each gospel narrates basically the same appearance, but every account varies because the authors felt free to adapt the non-essential elements of the story to fit their own purposes. It's also possible that there were a number of resurrection appearances and each locality and writer recorded the appearance which they felt was the most significant. But each account gives the impression that the disciples are seeing the risen Jesus for the first time. That's one reason why the attempts to provide a sequence of events which includes all the appearances is doomed to failure.

There's an interesting switch in the resurrection accounts. The earliest gospels, beginning with Mark, say very clearly that Jesus was raised up from the dead. Scripture scholars point out that this form of resurrection can be found in nineteen places in the New Testament. The idea in this earliest theology is that the Father raised Jesus from the tomb; the power of the Father is emphasized. In later traditions, particularly in the gospel of John, the concentration is upon Jesus: Jesus rose from the dead. The implication in this theology is that Jesus himself, by his own power, achieved a new resurrected life. John could do this because he developed a theology which spelled out the unity between the Father and the Son. But the first interpretation, namely that Jesus was raised up by the Father, is the understanding preferred by most Scripture scholars.

Reading through the various Resurrection episodes carefully will expose another problem. When did the ascension take place? And what is the connection between the Ascension and the Resurrection? The view held by most people is that the Ascension occurred forty days after the Resurrection. This number forty comes from the Acts of the Apostles. But the number forty is generally a symbolic indication of time, not a literal one. Besides, Luke, the author of the Acts, in his own gospel does not refer to a forty-day time lapse between the Resurrection and the Ascension. He implies in the gospel that the Ascension took place on Easter. This is certainly the implication in Mark's gospel. It's quite legitimate therefore, to think of the Ascension as occurring on Easter. Jesus is described as ascending "up" to heaven. This is symbolic language, and we need not think of heaven as "up." Speaking theologically, it is most probably accurate to say that Jesus, through his resurrection, was glorified by the Father and that Jesus appeared to his disciples as already glorified. In this view, the Passion, death, Resurrection, and Ascension of Jesus is considered one action, undergone for the salvation of man. It is one process, one movement. All four of those events are intimately connected, and one cannot be interpreted apart from the other three. Theologically, then, the time between the Resurrection and the Ascension does not make much difference, but the interval of forty days seems very unlikely.

There are accounts of other resurrections in the gospels. Lazarus and the daughter of Jairus are two examples. But these people died again. Jesus rose to a life of never dying again. His existence then after the Resurrection is not an "ordinary one." In fact, the New Testament records that some of his disciples did not recognize Jesus immediately. Jesus had changed; he was somehow different. And yet it was Jesus; the testimony is that they did see Jesus. There is therefore an element of change in Jesus as well as an element of continuity. The same Jesus changed in the process of Resurrection-Ascension. St. Paul says that "it is sown a physical body; it is raised a spiritual body" (1 Cor. 15:12). We really don't know what a "spiritual body" is, but we can appreciate what Paul is trying to say. After the Resurrection, there are differences, but it is the same person.

So What?

To isolate one incident in a series of events is to cut off the real meaning of that incident. For example, American political policy is based upon the principles of democracy. This form of politics demands a system by which the people have an opportunity to express their wishes. In America this system is in operation most dramatically every four years when the people elect their president. The actual election is one incident, taking place on one day. But to isolate that one day, considering only what happens at the polls on election day, is to miss the most significant aspects of that event. To know what really goes on at election time in America, an interested observer would have to analyze the mood of the country, the issues that have been prominent for months and probably years previous to the election, and the hopes people have for the future. He would also have to study the positions each candidate holds, the interests of the groups who support him, the past performance of the man, his personality, his style of leadership. To really understand the American political process at election time, an individual must put together many factors from the past and the present, and approach the results of an election with that information. Otherwise, the meaning of the election will remain basically incomprehensible.

A similar observation can be made regarding the Resurrection of Jesus. To isolate the Resurrection from the rest of the life and death of Jesus is to lose much of the meaning of the event. Unfortunately, there is a tendency to approach the Resurrection from this isolationist point of view. In this unbiblical approach, the Resurrection is seen as the greatest of Jesus' miracles. It is used as a proof of his divinity in arguments against those who deny that divinity. The resurrection, in this sense, is the "blue chip" proof; it can stand by itself, isolated and unrelated to the rest of the gospel message. In this viewpoint, the Resurrection is used as an indicator of something else, namely, the divinity of Jesus. It is taking the Resurrection out of its scriptural context and is similar to concentrating solely on an election day without regard to the complete political process.

A more accurate, scriptural approach to the resurrection is to view that final event in the context of the whole life of Jesus. The life, the preaching, the Passion, the death, the Resurrection, and the Ascension of the Christ is one continual movement or process. We have said many times that according to Mark, Jesus is involved from the beginning in a hard fought battle between the forces of evil and the forces of good. This confrontation has been the basic message all along, and it's not surprising that the Resurrection is a crucial event in that continuous struggle. It's in that context that the significance of the Resurrection becomes clearer.

The Resurrection of Jesus guarantees the victory over evil. The condition for benefiting from the power of the victory is faith, a faith that lives, that is operable in our daily lives. It is that victory which Christians celebrate in the sacraments; each sacrament in its own way recalls the Resurrection and invites the believer to participate in the process of conquering evil and rejoicing in the triumph of good. A sacrament is an action, and a sign of the triumph of life over death, joy over suffering, forgiveness over sin, and the future over the past. A sacrament is an invitation to the participant to actively join in the process of extending the establishment of the reign of God. A sacrament is one of man's ways of uniting himself with the saving action of God, and one of God's ways of uniting himself with the lives of men. And a sacrament restates the basic message of Mark—the reign of God is among us. We may not hear the message all the time, due either to our own ignorance and lack of faith or to the ambiguity and ineffectiveness in the way the sacrament is presented. But that message is there.

The sacraments are not the only signs of the reign of God and the triumph of good over evil. One way of looking at it is to say that wherever there is something good happening, there also is the power of God. One person helps another in need, offering him food, clothing, or a home

to live in, and the reign of God is further established. World leaders meet and propose a course of action which leads to greater peace on our planet, and the power of God is again in evidence. A flood destroys homes and uproots families, and people respond with food, money, and personal support to help the victims, and the Resurrection of Jesus is made manifest. A friend is troubled and worried, and someone listens to him, offering his affection and encouragement, and the message of the gospel is being preached. Justice is denied to a group of people, and yet some fight for greater justice and equal rights, and the ministry of the Christ is continued. There are multiple examples of good things happening. And wherever there is good, there is God; and wherever there is God, there is the struggle between the forces of good and evil; and wherever there is that struggle, there is the Resurrection of Jesus; and wherever there is the Resurrection, there is hope.

According to the gospel of Mark, the primary image of Jesus is not the crucified Messiah, but the risen Lord. Jesus is first and foremost risen and glorified. Christians then are "Resurrection people." They are people who marvel at the mystery of life, affirming the basic goodness of life, saying "yes" to creation, bowing their spirits in humble affection for the mysterious beauty that pervades existence. They are people who join the continuing fight against those forces which hold back the advancement of man, whether they be social, economic, psychological, or philosophical. They are people who serve others, meeting the needs of the socially downcast, the economically deprived, or the unloved. They are people who pray, who prophesy, who serve. And they are people who believe that the reign of God has been established by the saving action of the life, death, and resurrection of Jesus of Nazareth who has guaranteed the final victory of good over evil.